WHO IS THE REAL
BARBARA MANDRELL?

She's a member of a famous singing family, adored by
fans and press alike, a thorough professional who has
created an image that has carried her to the top—and kept
her there long after other stars have fallen in the night.
Here, for the first time, is a look into the heart of Barbara
Mandrell—whose perfectionism drove her to the edge of
collapse, whose perky smiles hid fear and depression after
a devastating auto accident shattered her body and soul; the
girl-next-door, who dared to marry for life and fight to
keep that love alive despite overwhelming odds. Meet her
for the first time in the book no fan can afford to miss:

*The
Barbara Mandrell
Story*

Berkley Books by Charles Paul Conn

THE BARBARA MANDRELL STORY
THE POSSIBLE DREAM
PROMISES TO KEEP:
   THE AMWAY PHENOMENON AND HOW IT WORKS
AN UNCOMMON FREEDOM
THE WINNER'S CIRCLE

THE
BARBARA MANDRELL
STORY

CHARLES PAUL CONN

BERKLEY BOOKS, NEW YORK

This Berkley book contains the complete
text of the original hardcover edition.
It has been completely reset in a typeface
designed for easy reading and was printed
from new film.

THE BARBARA MANDRELL STORY

A Berkley Book / published by arrangement with
the author

PRINTING HISTORY
G. P. Putnam's Sons edition / October 1988
Berkley edition / July 1989

ISBN: 0-425-11410-4

A BERKLEY BOOK ® TM 757,375
Berkley Books are published by The Berkley Publishing Group,
200 Madison Avenue, New York, NY 10016.
The name "BERKLEY" and the "B" logo
are trademarks belonging to Berkley Publishing Corporation.

PRINTED IN THE UNITED STATES OF AMERICA

10 9 8 7 6 5 4 3 2 1

*Dedicated to Ron Gilbert and
to Cheryl, Chris and Ryan*

Contents

Introduction

THE WARM SEPTEMBER evening was beginning to fade. Mark White, an avid hunter, had purchased his new bow shortly before 6:00 P.M. and flung it carelessly in the back seat of his station wagon. With only a few days remaining on his summer job, the University of Tennessee sophomore was gearing up to return to his math studies. The quiet nineteen-year-old edged his red 1980 Subaru onto US 31, west-bound toward Gallatin, Tennessee.

Inside the crowded Rivergate Mall, Matthew and Jaime Mandrell followed closely behind their mom in search of school clothes. Although she was going out West on tour the following morning, Barbara had taken time out to be with her kids. They finished shopping shortly after 6:00 P.M., and Barbara turned her silver 1980 Jaguar onto the four-lane highway, east-bound toward home.

Approaching a traffic light on the busy strip, the Mandrells observed three children perched precariously on the edge of a tailgate. The sight made the thirty-four-year-old country singer shudder; uncharacteristically, she and the kids immediately buckled up their seat belts.

The crash came without warning. The young student had swerved into Barbara's path. The Jaguar and Subaru met head-on at the combined speed of 100 miles per hour. Both cars crumpled like accordions.

Mark White lay dying. Ironically, the undamaged new hunting bow rested upright in the seat.

Although the lives of the Mandrells were certainly saved by their seat belts, the impact took its toll on each of them. Matthew sustained a broken nose and cheekbone as well as other internal injuries. Jaime had a number of bruises from the impact. Barbara lay semiconscious, moaning. Later examination would uncover a concussion, a fractured right leg, numerous lacerations and a broken ankle.

The task at hand, however, was to get everyone clear of the wreckage. Within minutes, the local rescue squad arrived and used the Jaws of Life to extricate the victims from the mangled automobiles. Traffic on the busy thoroughfare became snarled. Ironically, Irby Mandrell, Barbara's father and manager, was routed around the scene by police. Coming home from the singer's marina near Nashville, he was totally unaware of the tragedy. Louise Mandrell, summoned by the police, arrived on the scene in front of the Bluegrass Country Club just in time to accompany her sister on the short ride to Hendersonville Hospital. All were admitted. Mark White was pronounced DOA.

As Barbara was being removed from the ambulance, Louise covered her sister's face with a sheet. This added to the growing speculation about the seriousness of her injuries. Was she grossly disfigured or dying? Pressing back the reporters, Louise cried out, "She's been there for you. Now be there for her!" Barbara's fate would become a closely guarded secret until the full extent of her injuries could be determined.

Hendersonville and Gallatin are Nashville's classy backyard. Home of many noted country stars, they are counterparts to California's Beverly Hills. The real estate surrounding Hendersonville Lake has burgeoned into a sprawling complex of malls, eateries and posh subdivisions. The elite of the country music industry live and play here, with easy access to Nashville's "Music Row"—a street with music publishers and music clubs—by interstate highway.

The news about the perky blonde singer, musician, TV entertainer and superstar spread quickly through the tight-knit community of entertainers. Barbara Mandrell, veteran of hundreds of thousands of miles of road tours, now lay severely injured. She and her neighbors were people who made their living on the road. It seemed difficult to accept that something so tragic could happen so close to home.

An outpouring of support began to flow in from neighbors, as well as from loyal fans. Johnny Cash called, along with many other celebrities. Ralph Emery, a country talk-show host, well-known locally, came to the hospital. A flood tide of mail, flowers and phone calls began to inundate the hospital as news leaked out.

Realizing the severity of her injuries, Barbara's physicians made the decision to transfer her to Baptist Hospital in Nashville, where more sophisticated facilities were available for the kind of treatment she was going to need.

By this time, Ken Dudney, Barbara's husband of seventeen years, had been notified. He had been away on business in Spokane, Washington, and caught the first available plane home.

At Baptist, orthopedic surgeon Ray Jones was on the scene trying to put the pieces back together. He described Barbara's right leg injuries as "a jigsaw puzzle."

The tiny singer lingered on the threshold of consciousness. At one point she began pummeling the doctors with her fists, screaming, "You people don't touch me! Get away from me! I'll get my father in here!" Although she was dazed and disoriented, the intensity of Barbara's fighting spirit was beginning to show through. Later, while watching the hospital television alone, she would learn the fate of Mark White.

She regained consciousness to find a twelve-inch metal rod inserted in the bone marrow of her right leg. In the coming months, she would undergo major surgery several times and lie for weeks in traction. She would suffer memory loss, severe headaches, confusion and bouts of crying and depression.

Only one year earlier, she had presented a version of her dazzling Las Vegas show, "The Lady Is a Champ," to the hometown folks. It had been a smash. Showed her versatility and her intensity. It was the same intensity, the same exuberance that had launched the career of Barbara Jean Mandrell at the age of eleven when, perched behind a steel guitar at a Chicago trade show, she exuded a strong will to succeed. In the coming days, she would have to prove that she was indeed a champ. In order to guarantee that the museum she had built to immortalize her career would not prematurely become a mausoleum, the Lady would have to do it all over again.

The marquee outside the Barbara Mandrell Country Museum says "Come on in and be dazzled." The doors of the flag-lined building open into a glass-plated structure housing the essence of what it means to be Barbara Mandrell. The museum is a far cry from the stereotypical image of what country music is supposed to look like. Despite its attempt at a folksy, almost self-consciously homespun style, it is an example of first-rate marketing. Planted right in the middle of the Music Row complex, it draws visitors from all over the country. And they return again and again.

The tourist spot promises an alluring attraction: One gets the sense of being able to meet the real Barbara Mandrell here. All the trappings of success are displayed for her fans, like a warehouse made into a giant scrapbook: Here's the first Rolls-Royce; an impressive number of trophies, artifacts, mementos; crayon sketches; pictures of the early years. The stuff of a successful musical career—musical instruments, records, costumes, clippings—abounds. And all of it is arrayed with calculated taste and a canny eye for visitor response.

The Barbara Mandrell Country Museum is, above all else, entertaining, like the woman whose spirit dominates the place. Barbara's voice narrates the exhibits. One can watch her dance on videotape, and hear her sing on her old records. The curious can even see an exact replica of the bedroom where she and Ken sleep, right down to the crackers and soda can on the table. It is, as it was meant to be, the total Mandrell experience.

But despite the obvious care with which the museum has been assembled, it doesn't achieve the homespun feel that has been attempted. It's more Art Deco than barn dance, more chic than calico. It's glitzy, a reflection of Barbara's personal taste. There is glamor here, glamor with a diffused, soft glow-pastel kind of touch. The impression created is chic and sultry. Glass cases and recessed lighting fixtures convey an image easily associated with Barbara, and her touch is evident everywhere. One senses she has been here, changing this and that, arranging and rearranging, giving orders to the youthful workers. Many of them relate stories of the times she came and worked through the night for her fans. They recount what it is like to be with Ms. Mandrell.

Through all the glitz, the Lady still shines through. Even so, nothing here seems fully to have captured her essence, her elegance, intensity or determination, not even the books and glossy prints for sale in the souvenir stand. The litany of adjectives that have been used to describe her is familiar: trim, polished, tiny, petite, gorgeous, stunning. Yet familiar as they are, they fall short, as do the photographs that capture the image but not the essence of Barbara Mandrell.

The whole exhibit reflects a carefully sculpted image. It is an image honed by the star herself through years in the business, by such professionals as her publicist Jeannie Ghent and her agent JoAnn Berry, and by a family who knew about show biz and made it work for them.

But what about the woman it is meant to celebrate? Who is she? And what is she *really* like?

1

The Beginning

BORN IN HOUSTON, Texas, on Christmas Day of 1948, Barbara Mandrell seems to have been preparing her show-business image all her life. Her parents, Irby and Mary Mandrell, molded Barbara, and later her sisters, along these lines from their earliest years.

Irby Matthew Mandrell was a musician and would try to get the "boys" together to play whenever he had a chance. He had spent his teen years picking the guitar and singing on a country radio show in Hot Springs, Arkansas.

The desire to perform remained even after he married Mary Ellen McGill. She, too, had been part of a musical family. Mary, her brother Ira and sister-in-law Marjorie functioned as a gospel singing trio at the Pentecostal church where Ira pastored. Mary served as pianist, organist and music teacher.

The future couple met while Irby was traveling as a musician. He came to Ira's small country church in Illinois one Sunday and was immediately taken by Mary. They married soon after, on November 15, 1947.

The deep religious roots of the Mandrells were evident during the weeks prior to Barbara's birth. Mary lay unconscious, suffering from convulsions. Mary's physicians told Irby that his wife would need special surgery. They felt there was a chance they could save his wife, but the child's survival looked doubtful. Happily, Christmas Day of 1948 found the Mandrells singing "Happy Birthday" not only to their newborn daughter but to Baby Jesus as well. She had come into a family that was deeply committed to the fundamental beliefs of Christianity.

Irby was working steadily, as a policeman, when the baby was born. This afforded Barbara a relatively normal childhood, with one special addition: She was exposed constantly to a powerful love of music.

Mary taught her daughter to sing and play the accordion. As Barbara once said, "I learned to read music before I could read English." She knew the words and music to hymns almost before she could walk. Irby's passion for music also was transmitted to his daughter. "When she gets an ovation, part of it is mine," he has said.

Barbara often refers to her sisters Louise and Irlene as her best friends. But that wasn't always so. When Barbara was five, Louise came along and Barbara was not thrilled. She recalls that her dad took her to the hospital to see the new arrival. Irby teased the slightly jealous Barbara by claiming he was not sure that this was really her baby sister because her hair was so dark. He threatened to flush the baby down the toilet. Barbara pleaded and pleaded. He finally relented, after she promised to take good care of the infant. Barbara became a miniature mom for Louise, who was born in 1954, and eighteen months later for Irlene.

Barbara's vocal debut also came in 1956, when she played a well-known hymn on the accordion in church.

The folks liked it so much, she played it again—and was hooked.

Irby was now a regional sales manager for the Standel Amplifier Company. The family moved often, but they were always surrounded by people who loved music. When Barbara was of school age, the family moved to Ocean-side, California. Irby opened a music store with partner Bill Hendrick, who later played sax for the family band. The Mandrells lived in a house trailer. After school and on weekends, Barbara and her sisters began to work out on the variety of instruments stocked in the store.

Even in school, Barbara loved to perform. Her teachers recall that she would present reports from the front of the class rather than from her seat. On the back of one report card it was noted that she was "bossy." Another teacher noted she would make a great PTA president.

By the time Barbara reached the fifth grade, she was proficient on the banjo, steel guitar and saxophone. A *Saturday Evening Post* interview (April 1982) with Barbara revealed that one day she came home with a declining grade in math: "Dad asked [the teacher] how I was doing in music, and she understood I was getting an A. Then he asked if I was learning enough math to figure percentages, and she said yes, she thought so. He asked if I knew how to count money and again the answer was yes. He said, 'Good. All I ever expected was for her to learn music, figure percentages and count money.' "

At times, her parents literally had to take the instruments away and make Barbara go outside and play. These were the early days of rockabilly and rock and roll and she loved the music. Nor, a little later, was she immune to the magic of the Beatles. No doubt these influences, leavened by a healthy infusion of the Memphis sound and Motown, left their mark on the future star.

All over the South and West, radio stations carried the Grand Ole Opry every Saturday night, and the Mandrell clan could be numbered among the audience of faithful listeners.

Barbara's early accordion repertoire went beyond country music. It included the old favorite "Lady of Spain" as well as pop tunes. She kept learning, practicing, playing.

Her big break came at the tender age of eleven. She had begun to add pedal steel lessons to the rest of her varied musical activities. She was doing so well on steel that Irby decided to take her with him to the Palmer House in Chicago. This was the scene for a trade fair, and Barbara was given the opportunity to help demonstrate Standel amplifiers.

Country Joe Maphis was there and liked what he saw and heard. He knew what other folks liked too. Irby's perky blonde daughter was a show-biz natural. He immediately signed her for the Showboat nightclub in Las Vegas.

Looking back on the experience, Barbara remembers how she was legally too young to have been allowed in the club. She was given a strict route to follow to get to the dressing room and stage; she wasn't allowed to go anyplace else. Dutifully, she did as she was told, with Irby right there by her side.

Later in 1960, she made her first television appearance in Los Angeles on a show called *Town Hall Party*. She became a regular feature. It was a grind for the young performer—the show was four hours long and was filmed live—but public response was overwhelming. As always, they loved the smiling young girl playing the steel guitar.

That success breeds success couldn't be more true when it comes to American show business. Accordingly, soon after the Las Vegas success, Barbara made her first network debut on ABC on a show called *Five Star Jubilee*. It originated in Springfield, Missouri, and was hosted by Rex Allen. She was now all of twelve years old.

These opportunities brought her into contact with some of the hottest country music greats. She took to the road with such stars as Johnny Cash, Tex Ritter and Red Foley. She made friends with Patsy Cline and toured briefly with her. Thankfully, circumstances kept her from joining the ill-fated flight that took the lives of Patsy and Cowboy Copas.

Irby started the Mandrell Family Band when Barbara was fourteen. This was an idea born out of self-defense and the desire to keep his family together. Barbara had been on the road more and more often. His other girls were growing up, and he wanted a vehicle in which to showcase the skills that he and Mary had fostered. Irby played guitar and sang while Mary played bass. Barbara was featured, showing her versatility on steel guitar, saxophone and banjo.

At the outset, a drummer was needed. It would be several years before baby Irlene would take to the sticks. A twenty-two-year-old grocery store clerk auditioned. He was hired and traveled with the group for four years. His name was Ken Dudney and he eventually would become Barbara's husband.

The road was a never-ending procession of one-night stands: Lions Clubs, county fairs, even military bases and hospitals. But the grind was valuable to Barbara, allowing her continuously to refine her ability to please and entertain. Meeting other musicians also was an education in itself. Absorbing their styles, learning their licks, Barbara was insatiable, constantly growing. And, whether consciously or not, she was developing the Mandrell style, winning the hearts of legions of future fans and polishing the persona, the image that would become her trademark.

It's never easy being a child-star. The scrap heap of those who could not adapt is piled high with the wreckage of careers, families, even lives. Thàt Barbara managed it at all is remarkable. The extraordinary thing about her is that she did it so well.

She appeared on local television. She was on the radio. She began recording on the Mosrite label. She traveled, and played incessantly. She was everywhere. Through it all, she kept up with her school work. An outstanding student, she ran track, played ball and served on the student council. Of course, she also played in the school band and sang in the choir.

She was now in that awful transition period from childhood to adulthood. She was no longer applauded for just being "cute." It was apparent that her enormous talent was emerging. Audiences recognized it and responded. Others in the business saw it too.

At age sixteen, she won the Miss Oceanside Beauty Contest easily. Barbara's beauty and talent were unbeatable— as was her self-assurance. She told writer Holly Miller in the April 1982 *Saturday Evening Post* interview that "the girls backstage complained their hands were sweaty because they were so scared. I couldn't understand or sympathize because I'd never had butterflies. I'd been working since I was eleven in front of the public, and it was no big deal to me. The only time I really suffered stage fright was when I was going down the aisle to be married. I told my dad, 'So this is what it feels like . . .' "

The Mandrells' burgeoning involvement in entertaining at military installations opened some new doors. The family was invited to entertain overseas. This was during the Vietnam conflict, and they were eager to serve, making their first tour to Hawaii in 1964. In 1966 and 1967, they played to servicemen in the Philippines, Japan and Thailand.

Vietnam provided the group with the experience of entertaining in areas of combat operations, and gave the soldiers a taste of the high-octane Mandrell energy. After the shows, members of the audience would come up to the performers with tears in their eyes. The music had taken them back home again, away from the reality of war and, once again, loyal fans were recruited, many of whom remain faithful today.

Barbara was only fourteen when Irby hired her future husband. Ken Dudney says he was attracted to her during the first Mandrell Family Band photo session, when he was introduced to Barbara. The group was together constantly during those years, especially in the summer and on weekends.

At first, he cautiously approached Irby about taking all three girls out together, but soon he was dating Barbara. They began to talk of marriage. He bought a wedding ring long before they actually set a date and had just about finished paying it off when Mary discovered her daughter wearing it.

By 1967, Vietnam was raging. After visiting there on tour, Ken decided to enlist. He joined the Navy and soon qualified for pilot training. The Mandrells figured that would be the end of things. Barbara thought so too. After about a year, however, Ken called and asked if he could take her to church on a Sunday.

They picked up where they had left off. Ken formally proposed. Barbara accepted on the condition that they would wait until she finished high school. The wedding took place one week before she received her diploma. They were able to be together for about ten days before he was shipped back overseas.

The Navy ensign's bride moved back home, only to

discover the family was moving again. Irby's brother lived in Dyersburg, Tennessee, and was interested in going into the construction business. The family decided to give it a try.

The Mandrells packed up and relocated in Newbern, Tennessee, where Barbara and the rest of the clan attempted to settle down to a new life. She traded her steel guitar for pots and pans.

Her attempt at homemaking was short-lived. Irby's new job required him to travel, and he would often take the whole family along in a trailer. On one very special trip, in 1968, they went to Nashville and visited the Grand Ole Opry in the old Ryman Auditorium. Things were cooking: It was crowded and hot. The main floor had support posts that hampered the view of many of the less fortunate ticket holders. But as was often the case, the place had an electric effect upon those who aspired to its stage. This was to become a benchmark in Barbara's life—her first visit to the Parthenon of country music.

The young housewife and former child-star whispered to her father during the performance, "Daddy, if you've got any faith in me, I'd like to try to get on the other side of the microphone again. I wasn't cut out to be in the audience." Irby agreed to manage her.

Close to her twentieth birthday, Barbara's new career was launched. With Irby as her manager, the Nashville newcomer booked a spot at a nightclub in the now defunct Printer's Alley, a seamy strip of watering holes near the Ryman Auditorium. The legendary country greats hung out there to catch the local talent.

It seemed almost too easy. In one night, Barbara's steel pickin' netted her six different offers. One young manager who would play a key role in her meteoric rise to stardom would be Billy Sherrill of Columbia Records. Sensing a winner, he convinced Irby to let her sign her first major recording contract.

The period of the late sixties was rife with protest, political dissent and revolutionary spirit—in music as well as politics. Even though rock and roll was still king, change was in the wind. Few performers seemed able to command public attention for very long. Elvis and a select group were continually on the charts, but the public seemed weary of the "new" heavy sounds and the perpetual parade of new talent presented to them. Things had somehow lost their innocence.

In this context, the rebirth of country music was inevitable. But who could have predicted the incredible number of mainline rock stations that would be jumping ship a decade later? An unprecedented number switched to an all-country format for the simple reason that it was in their best commercial interests.

At the same time, the Nashville sound itself was changing. It had become more sophisticated, more demanding, and seemed to offer a new dimension to the listeners. New technologies were available to the performers who, themselves, had bold new perspectives. Like their rock and roll counterparts, they reflected a nation in the throes of rapid evolution. Questioning the status quo was almost a prerequisite for success in the music industry. And Barbara Mandrell was right there in the middle of it!

The new country sound was slicker, more polished. So was the new Barbara Mandrell. Her greatest gift seemed to be her ability to "read" the crowd. She knew what they wanted and responded to. She knew that people like variety. She sensed their restlessness, and decided to change her style.

With Billy Sherrill producing for her, she began to experiment, evolving a sound that was part soul, part country. Almost single-handedly, she created a slick, smooth hybrid of the best music of Memphis and Motown. The new sound was mellow, the rough edges of its forebears rubbed smooth. It didn't take long for the new "homogenized" country style to catch on with other entertainers as well, but Barbara was one of the first to cash in on its popularity. She was suddenly popular in the grand show-business sense of the word. Most of all, she was immensely marketable.

Being "discovered" a second time brought new advantages. Barbara began her new career on March 1, 1969, at CBS. Her first hit was an old Otis Redding tune, "I've Been Loving You Too Long." The public loved it.

Countless appearances followed. She toured extensively to promote her new music. When the Grand Ole Opry opened its stage to her, the first part of her new dream was complete. At last she stood on the other side of the microphone. She was filling the shoes of a succession of country music legends.

Barbara had by now become more polished, more loved, more versatile—and more determined. The Memphis/Detroit/Nashville alliance enabled her to crank out a string of tunes destined to take her to the top. Her eclectic style was called "middle-of-the-road." It would help bring a rash of new country fans on board.

She was on an upward spiral from 1969 to 1973, but making a significant breakthrough wasn't easy. It required miles of road work and hundreds of one-night stands.

"If Loving You Is Wrong," "Do-Right Woman" and a steady stream of other hits helped her put the wheels on her future. Touring began regularly once again. The money began to flow in to stem the tide of debt that goes with launching a career.

The worst aspect of those trying times was being away

from Ken. The first struggling steps had to be taken without his support. Irby was still a rock, but the young bride missed her new husband.

Emblematic of her situation is the time she planned an impromptu visit to Ken while he was stationed in France. She contacted him and made arrangements. He booked her into a posh hotel on the French Riviera.

Ken wasn't sure which plane she would be on and ended up missing her. After several flights had come and gone, he gave up. He headed back for the ship, sixty miles away.

Meanwhile, Barbara looked out from the plane on her approach to the Nice airport. The USS *Independence* was clearly visible from the air. She was so excited. She hadn't seen Ken in months. However, when she landed, no one was there to meet her.

Unable to speak French, she tried desperately to get a taxi, but to no avail. She finally ended up on a bus headed in the general direction of the ship. Naturally, she missed her stop.

At the corner, she flagged down a couple of Navy shore patrolmen and told them she was "the wife of Ensign Kenneth Dudney of the carrier *Independence*." They directed her to the pier where she could catch a launch to the ship. Her odyssey continued.

Luckily Ken, traveling back from the airport, spotted her on the pier. It was a happy but short-lived reunion. The original hotel reservations had been surrendered, and now it was difficult to find a place to stay. They settled for a room on the seamier side of the city. It had no shower and no toilet. It did have plenty of "hostesses" who quietly entertained guests in their rooms. But it really didn't matter. What did matter was that the Dudneys were together again.

After this second honeymoon, Barbara contacted an agent who had told her she might be able to get some concerts in Europe. To her surprise, she found she had been booked for seventeen appearances in Germany, at over $100 a night. When she rejoined Ken a few weeks later in Genoa, she laid her earnings out on the bed—$1,700! They had never seen so much money.

The news of the arrival of their first child prompted Ken to leave the service. Barbara sought the advice of her doctor about the special dilemma her lifestyle presented. He supported her feeling that the child was going to have to adapt, as part of a family that happened to earn a living from the road. Barbara thought it best to bring the child up in this way, in an environment she so loved.

Matthew born in 1970 began touring with his mom when he was just six weeks old. The rest of the children, Jaime born in 1976 and Nathaniel born in 1985, have done the same.

Determination and hard work had shaped Barbara's early career. Building and growing had become natural processes. The years between 1973 and 1979 were significant because the foundations of her empire were being laid. Commercial success had brought her important new contacts.

The revitalized career was not without its bad moments, however.

Things were not always as slick as she tried to make them. Take the case of her first Fan Fair. This is the premier event for country music fans. All the stars converge in Nashville at the fairgrounds every summer for three days of singing, concerts and autographing sessions. The musicians try to generate publicity and attend photo opportunities for the fans, working hard to create the sense of the personal touch. They give dozens of interviews, offering amiable cooperation whether they feel like it or not. All of this activity has a single purpose—increasing record sales and ratings.

Barbara painfully remembers that first fair. No one knew her. Instead of the excitement of crowds shouting requests for autographs, she had little more than three solid days of standing around, waiting between sets. She says she just loves it now because she is so busy with the fans. Back then, it wasn't so.

This was all the more reason to keep at it. The relentless singer forged on. She booked more tours, concerts and fair dates. Every engagement made her a little stronger, brought her a little closer to the people. Her image and stage presence were sharpened and she became even more dazzling. Her reputation as a top-notch performer was starting to get around.

Barbara's interests went beyond the on-stage performance. She saw the way her profession had organized itself in unions and associations. She also noticed that the organizations did not seem to reflect the changing patterns of country music, so she got involved in another, more political way. Eventually, she was elected a board member of the Academy of Country Music. It was time to recognize the achievements of those like herself, those who did not fit within the standard categories that had been defined so long ago.

Such talents as John Denver and Olivia Newton-John were considered stepchildren of the industry back then. Barbara's efforts forced the Academy to include a more diverse cross-section of singers in its ranks. She had helped pioneer this new sound; it was only fitting that she be involved in its institutionalization. This led to the establishment of a splinter group called the Country Music Association, in 1974.

Of course, this led to a raging controversy. Hers was not

really "country" music, some argued. It was a mongreliza-
tion, a perversion of "pure" art.

Barbara never broke stride. She continued to focus on
her innovative music, "countrified" rather than "country." The style included bits and pieces of the trends that
were popular in the larger world of music. Deviating from
the original Nashville sound, songs such as "Woman to
Woman" and "Married But Not to Each Other" blended
traditional country with rhythm and blues.

Despite her rebellious streak, however, Barbara was still
a traditionalist at heart, in some ways even straightlaced.
She performed the raunchier traditional "skin songs" of
the industry stock and trade antiseptically, with Sunday
School fervor. After all, this was a family act. Her dad
drove the bus. Louise played the bass.

The bus turned out to be a haven for Barbara. The
standards she commanded away from home seemed in-
congruent with what was going on in the rest of the
industry. She banned groupies, liquor and drugs from the
bus. She named her band the Do-Rites, after her 1970 hit
of the same name.

Business was booming and required a support system.
Mary stayed behind, manning the phones and booking
dates. Ken was a pilot for the state of Tennessee, ferrying
the Governor to his appointments. He also began to manage the money now flowing into the Mandrell coffers, and
has continued to function in this role to the present.

Of course, Barbara took a few days off to have Jaime,
her second child, in 1976. The night before, she was
performing at the Opry, into which she had been officially
inducted in 1972.

In 1976, another major change occurred when she made
the switch to ABC (MCA) records. Her next hit tune,
"Standing Room Only," assured her place as America's

top country ballad singer. The unique niche she had created began to pay off. "That's What Friends Are For" (1976), "Love Is Thin Ice" (1976) and "Woman to Woman" (1977) all were hit singles. An album, "The Best of Barbara Mandrell" (1977), captured the highlights of the past years of hard work and the fans responded enthusiastically.

In 1978, "Sleeping Single in a Double Bed" hit the top of the country charts and held for three weeks. It then crossed over into the pop world and climbed higher. "If Loving You Is Wrong (I Don't Want to Be Right)" (1979) hit the charts in the top third and once again made it into the pop charts. Homogenized waves of similar tunes soon followed. "Midnight Angel" (1979), "Fooled by a Feeling" (1979), "You Can Eat Crackers in My Bed" (1980), "Best of Strangers" (1980).

So much success had come so soon. Yet Barbara learned early that along with the glamor and the lights come the critics. This is probably the area in which the entire Mandrell organization has responded least well. The singer with the carefully sculptured image finds it difficult to take professional or personal criticism easily.

Barbara's performances have been called "too supperclub slick" by the *Illustrated Encyclopedia of Country Music*. This image tended to alienate some who preferred more mainstream country.

In Los Angeles, KLAC program director Don Langford has likened her to the "soft side of Dolly Parton and a little bit of Emmylou Harris with strings." She does like the fat sound that violins provide. Some also complain that her stage act is a bit too "mushy" and sentimental between tunes. *People* magazine went so far as to dub her "Country Music's Snow White" (February 14, 1977) and noted that she has draped herself in "mink and morality."

She found herself reading every word written about her.

She admits that in the beginning she was skeptical of what writers said, especially if it was negative. One particular columnist said she talked too much between songs. She disagreed. After reviewing tapes of the concert, she reluctantly accepted the criticism as valid. Despite her sensitivity to criticism, even today she maintains a scrapbook. It gives her perspective, she says.

Despite the carping of the critics, and the cynicism of outsiders, there is a generosity of spirit in Barbara Mandrell. She has earned her success, and she knows it. But she also knows that she couldn't have done it without help.

Barbara has often acknowledged the influence of her family in the success she has had. Uncle Ira had deep musical as well as spiritual influences. She acknowledges several teachers who made their mark on her. One was Norman Hamlet, who later played steel guitar for Merle Haggard. Another was A. R. Lambson, her high school choir director. Certainly, her mother was an integral part of Barbara's successes. Her father, still her manager, ranks up there at the top.

Alongside the many plaques in the Dudney/Mandrell residence today is one that symbolizes this last debt. It reads: "Thanks for letting me help one of my dreams come true. DAD."

In spite of the critics, Barbara still had a loyal following by the end of the 1970s. The sound was polished. The act was together. She had several hit albums and singles, and toured the nation in a forty-foot Prevost bus. What could possibly be left for Barbara Mandrell to accomplish?

2

New Horizons

BARBARA MANDRELL WAS not a stranger to TV. From her earliest days on *Town Hall Party* and *Five Star Jubilee,* she had shown she had the magic. Sometimes the TV camera doesn't like what it sees. No matter how talented or entertaining a person may be, if the chemistry isn't there, it just won't work. But it has always worked for her.

The television camera liked the way Barbara looked. People were beginning to notice that fact as she made more frequent appearances in 1978 and 1979: on *Today* and on the Dinah Shore, Mike Douglas, and Tom Snyder shows. She touched all the standard bases for a rising star. Hollywood began to clamor for more.

Even in the days of black-and-white, the monochrome image was able somehow † capture her verve, her talent. People who saw her sensed that she would someday become a star, though no one then could have guessed where TV was headed, nor could anyone have predicted the potential commercial success of country music. But when

Barbara worked the two in tandem, she found she could create a sensation. She's done it ever since.

To understand the unique set of circumstances that propelled the Mandrells to the forefront of American entertainment requires an overview of the dynamics prevailing at that time in the rest of the nation.

In the late seventies, the American public seemed to be tilting in a more conservative direction. The elections were about to give the Republicans a wide margin in government. Things were swinging back toward more traditional values. At the same time, technology was changing. Satellite dishes began to pop up like mushrooms in backyards everywhere. These provided an enormous impetus to the entertainment industry, both negative and positive. Some media figures feared a loss of network control by allowing signals to be openly transmitted. What would happen to the ratings? Others saw enormous potential in the phenomenon and set out to exploit it.

Barbara had been working the television circuit for years; she had paid her dues. But at the time there was not enough push from the top to provide a berth for country music as a regular television feature. Certainly, she was good enough. She had the act, and at least as much talent as the mainstays, though that doesn't seem to matter much to the media decision-makers. But the time was fast approaching when the public would demand to see more of her. These were the early days of cable and other forms of pay TV. Again, there was a revolution of sorts and the Mandrells seemed to be waiting in the wings.

It was the dawn of the grand unseating of the network greats. Plans were on the drawing board to implement an all-country music network, which would capitalize on the influx of new talent coming to prominence, as well as provide an outlet for established Grand Ole Opry stars.

The new network and other similar ventures would also be a boon to sales and marketing of records throughout the music industry.

In 1979, however, there were as yet no champions of country music in mainstream TV strongholds. The Osmonds, a generic all-American family, were the most recent musical act to appeal successfully to family-oriented viewers. But aside from an occasional toe-tapping banjo tune, their shows featured little country music.

The general state of television was in question. Critics from all corners were arguing about the quality of network television programming. Groups of media activists sprang up in all parts of the country. Arguing from every part of the political spectrum, they put television fare under a powerful microscope. And they found something to offend nearly everybody. Investigations into TV violence were conducted by the government.

To those with foresight, this turmoil held great potential. Movies such as *Urban Cowboy* had helped. Pickup trucks were in. So was dressing like cowboys and riding mechanical bulls. After all, this was true American expression. It was an art form, indigenous only to the US of A.

The medium of broadcasting is not new to country music. The two have always been closely intertwined. In fact, country music was one of the first to utilize radio. In 1925, radio station WSM began broadcasting the Grand Ole Opry. This makes it one of the most celebrated and longest running shows in media history. It also helps to account for the long-term commitment of fans to the music.

Country is truly an American creation, with roots in a multitude of other cultures. If one is not an aficionado, it is difficult to accept the merits of country's claim to the respect due an art form. But like jazz, to which it is related, it remains an authentic part of our heritage.

In the late twenties and into the Great Depression, the audience for country grew steadily, as more and more people began to obtain radio sets for their homes. Across vast, lonesome stretches of the countryside, farmers, workers and kids dreaming of success were listening to legends such as Roy Acuff and Lester Flatt, along with the other members of the ensemble that now makes up the Country Music Hall of Fame.

Consider the effects the new technology of radio had on mass culture: It colored the way Americans related to each other, the way they talked, sang, danced, courted and dressed. And country music was the only cultural form that was presented. WSM and other stations, such as WWVA of Wheeling, West Virginia, went a long way to generate a kindred spirit among listeners. Whole new worlds were opened up in the Midwest and the Plains, where the accessibility of other forms of entertainment was so limited. The musical influences from the great state of Texas were strongly fueled by means of the broadcasts from far away.

The laborers, miners and workers from the coalfields found solace in radio. It was a poor man's therapy. One didn't have to hit Broadway to kick back and enjoy. But it was much more than the simple turn of a dial: Family listening time quickly became an event, then a ceremony and, finally, an institution.

The explosion of country music, and its ever widening influence, all took place in the old Ryman Auditorium. Built in 1899 as a church by a riverboat captain, it became the scene of concerts and eventually the first home of WSM's weekly broadcast. When one visits it today, there is still a special feeling there. Maybe one senses the ghosts of those now in hillbilly heaven who still hang around. To any performer who ever sang or played there, Ryman still holds great meaning.

Hank Williams, Ernie Ford, Ernest Tubb, Lester Flatt, Patsy Cline, Cowboy Copas, Stringbean—they all would tell you the Ryman was special. It had an almost carnival flavor, a spirit reminiscent of the old barn dances. There was nothing fancy about it. Yet it helped launch so many and bring so much to America.

The auditorium is now located in an area full of urban decay and upheaval. But all around there are new signs of progress, renovation and renewal. Maybe that is a sign of what this place really did for so many and a fitting repayment of an incalculable cultural debt.

Today the Ryman is a shrine. It has long been a mecca for country fans, and many still make the pilgrimage. The new Opry House is a posh structure, located several miles away on the Opryland grounds. It has facilities for first-rate productions and broadcasts. Yet, for some, the old place *was* the Opry, and it is gone forever.

If radio had this overwhelming effect, in the very dawn of the electronic revolution, it is hard to imagine what effect TV and movies might ultimately have. If radio was capable of changing the national destiny, then certainly the satellite has the potential for an as yet unknowable influence on all of us.

Barbara Mandrell, in retrospect, becomes a pivotal character in the evolution of the medium. It is not just her TV show or her unique sense of music that is significant. The flowering of a different approach to TV programming seems fixed at about the time of her collision with the powers of network television. Whether she in some way caused these changes or was merely riding the wave of other, greater trends is arguable, but clearly she was there in the middle of it.

Before Barbara, the only "countrified" programs to make it in prime-time television were *Green Acres* and *Hee-Haw*. The success of the latter was primarily due to the miracle of syndication. Now one of the oldest running shows on TV, it had proved country culture was marketable on a mass scale. *Hee-Haw* was a property of Gaylord Broadcasting of Tulsa, Oklahoma. Gaylord went on to buy out Opryland USA and eventually wind up with ownership of The Nashville Network (TNN).

TNN is the largest operation of its kind. It boasts over thirty million viewers and operates eighteen hours a day. It is advertiser-supported and is distributed through Group W Satellite Communications. At the current time it is the only one of a handful of such specialty outlets to feature country music exclusively in its programming. The network has claimed over seventy full-fledged members of the Grand Ole Opry among its performers. Since its inception, over 4,000 hours of programming has been produced.

Entrepreneurs Elmer Alley, David Hall and Paul Griscom launched the concept in 1983. Owned and operated by Opryland, it was originally part of Opryland Productions, an organization that did freelance work in the early days. Music videos were still a thing of the future. Elmer Alley's dream was to create a vehicle that would spotlight the entire industry and promote the entire cultural spectrum centered in Nashville. Not confined to music, the network would actively produce game shows and variety shows as well. It would be a breeding ground for new talent. It would spotlight up-and-coming personalities. And, of course, it would foster lots of all-American tourism. There was nothing else like it. The success of *Hee-Haw* was an indicator that the viewers were out there waiting. Time proved them right, but at the beginning it was a major gamble. TNN hosted the first Farm Aid in 1985, and also broadcast its second anniversary from Radio City Music Hall. It is currently seen in all fifty states.

The network originates from the 400-plus acres of the Opryland complex. This is the site of the Opry itself, and also boasts a theme park and broadcast facilities. This staggering incarnation dwarfs the imagination of those who first dreamed of the concept, and it has all taken place within only a few years. The recent success of TNN notwithstanding, however, the prospect of a prime-time variety series devoted entirely to country music was an almost foolish risk in 1979.

Barbara continued to show she was capable of pulling it off. "Lucy Comes to Nashville," and finally a small speaking part in "Murder in Music City" kept her in the public eye. Since there was a dearth of freshness, of good, clean talent, network officials began to reconsider her potential. A transition might be possible. Why couldn't she be successful as a network regular, perhaps even become a household word?

One of the people who recognized Barbara's potential was Marty Krofft. Winning fame with brother Sid and their puppet wizardry, he used his leverage to promote an idea for a series built around Barbara and her music. "Variety is the thing we know best," Krofft stated in an AP wire story of March 22, 1981: "In 1975, we created and produced the last successful variety show—*Donny and Marie*. I'd been trying to get a country music variety show off the ground for years," he said. "The networks wouldn't listen. So when a fellow came to me and asked about putting together a show with Barbara Mandrell, I told him I couldn't guarantee him I could sell her. Not by herself anyway. I asked if she had any relatives that played or sang. He showed me this picture." The snapshot did it all. The three sisters had posed for a campy glamor pose.

After viewing tapes of a co-hosting stint on the Mike Douglas show, Krofft took a chance.

"I took the idea to ABC and CBS and they turned it down. Then I went to Saul Ilson and said, 'Saul, this is what I have.' I gave him the picture." Ilson was NBC's vice president in charge of variety and comedy.

"I know that Fred Silverman (then president of the network) didn't know the Mandrells, but he can see," Krofft related. "He looked at the photograph and said, 'If you can get them, you've got a pilot.' "

Marty took the news back to Barbara and told her that he couldn't guarantee success. She responded, "You don't have to . . . I never fail."

The original deal called for six shows to be aired in as many consecutive weeks on a Saturday night slot in the NBC lineup. The pilot had been a success. In May of 1981, Brandon Tartikoff, president of NBC Entertainment, said, "Its soul is country, but its appeal is far-reaching, going way beyond that of country music."

Tartikoff was just the latest passenger on the Mandrell bandwagon, which had been picking up steam for several years. And television was just the logical next step. In October of 1980, Barbara had won the coveted Country Music Association's Female Entertainer of the Year award. (She'd been nominated three times before and not won.) In an interview with Bob Banner of the *Nashville Banner* on October 24, 1980, she revealed: "I've been trying to keep calm. It's like being in the midst of a dream. It really is. I dreamed and I hoped. But it was such a shock. I'm thankful about it all. Right now, I'm savoring every moment that I can." She thanked the Country Music Association for "giving me the chance to do something that meant everything to me."

The years of trying and not winning had only made her try harder, culminating in her eventual success. She was at her peak. *Music City News* voted her Best Female Vocalist, and *Cashbox* singled her out as Female Entertainer of the Year, as well as top Female Vocalist/Country Singles. *Billboard* dubbed her hit "Sleeping Single in a Double Bed" the Single of the Year.

Irby Mandrell stayed active in the background. At one point, he nearly died of a heart attack while driving on tour. The bus had broken down and he was determined to see the girls through. It almost killed him. It was time to move up. Barbara felt as if they had all paid their dues. Maybe the TV show was the answer.

As so often in the past, the Mandrell sense of timing—in this case Barbara's emphasis on family—seemed to coincide with a national need. Barbara had always wanted to make a go of it professionally with her two siblings. The family had always stuck together. When they could perform and travel together, it was ideal. However, things just never seemed to go that way. There were always problems.

Louise had been traveling as a bass player. She started with Barbara, then formed her own band. This period was interlaced with personal difficulties stemming from two failed marriages. Eventually, Louise married country singer R. C. Bannon and things stabilized for her.

Irlene also had designs on show biz, but her oldest sister had always seemed to dwarf her efforts. Irlene was probably the least musical of the three, but she had finally taken up the drums along with singing and modeling, which was paying the bills in 1979. She was working in Nashville at the time, applying her genuine good looks to modeling assignments while also trading on Barbara's golden name. The formula was pretty good. Still, Barbara had hopes of forming a family band.

Prior to agreeing to do the television show, Barbara alluded in a newspaper interview (December 11, 1979) to two people very close to her who just couldn't seem to make it in the business: "They expected everything to come F-A-S-T." She concluded that these two people didn't have "the guts to stick it out." It's hard to tell from those remarks whether or not she was really referring to her sisters.

She later claimed one of the reasons for doing the show was to help her sisters. The family was performing together once more and they were ready for the big time. The country was ready too: The political climate extolled God and patriotism, faith and family. The Mandrells were perfect—wholesome but sexy, corny but cute, silly but slinky. They weren't plastic, and they weren't Hollywood. These were definite advantages in these reflexive, almost reactionary, times. They were a combination of all the best in currently celebrated values, and they were unique to television.

Barbara arrived in California to begin taping and the Mandrells leased a home near the studio so they could be together while working. She was now thirty-one.

Success could not be entirely guaranteed: Would her sometimes corny, often slick show connect with the larger viewing public, and could she make the switch to a mass invisible audience after communicating one-on-one in live appearances before the folks back home? Would the ratings hold? Or would the show just gobble up material and talent, quickly depleting the freshness and zest of the act?

Barbara expressed her reservations: "At first, I wasn't really excited about the idea of a series, although I had wanted to do one for a long time. After meeting with Sid and Marty Krofft, my producers, and Saul Ilson, who's the head of variety programming at NBC, what came down was the series. I spent an awful lot of time thinking about it, and I think it was just meant to be.'' She was her usual upbeat self: ''I'm very excited and feel very good about the series. I think it's a terrific opportunity and I know I'm going to enjoy working on the show. The people we've been talking with at NBC have been just fantastic and we're all going to give it our best shot.''

She described the show as half comedy and half music. ''It's going to be a variety show, so I'll have my country guests but we'll also have people from outside country music—which seems only fair to me. Why segregate kinds of music? I can't expect Tim Conway or Bob Hope to have country stars on their shows and then not have non-country guests on my show.''

Then as now, she was fan conscious. ''I talk to my fans all the time, so of course I talked to them about this. I feel like if I don't keep my line to them open I won't know what my boss wants me to do because they are really who I work for.''

She spent time praying about the series. ''When I was thinking all this through I finally just said, 'Okay, God, it's in your hands. You've got it.' I really prayed about this and I think it is really the right thing to do.''

Barbara Mandrell and the Mandrell Sisters premiered on November 18, 1980. The critics liked it, saying that it was entertaining and well-coordinated.

People magazine (February 9, 1981) likened it to a ''cross between *Hee-Haw* and *The Smothers Sisters*.''

The family's religious roots went deep into the core of the act. It was impossible to remove this aspect without diminishing the original intent of what Barbara was trying to do. The gospel song remained in the act, despite what some of the producers thought.

The show also brought to life the change for which she and others had worked so hard. The series gave a tangible boost to the "slick" new sound of country music. It showed the nation that the stereotypes they held about CW did not hold. It debunked the myths about the coarseness and lack of singing talent needed to make it as a country singer.

The early ratings confirmed what the Mandrells suspected. Nielsen put it in the top forty. The schedule was maintained in prime time. *TV Guide*'s Robert MacKenzie in his review stated: "[The series] shows where country western is today: Slick and showy, produced with finesse, retaining the folksiness but shucking the corn. The audience is no longer rural. . . . Accordingly, the music is detwanged, domesticated, and dressed up in full orchestration.

"[Barbara] includes a lot of the old CW standards and her guests are authentic artists who were playing the same stuff fifteen years ago when nobody cared."

When she reached the number-one spot, the star's first question was how they played in Nashville. The fact was, they were playing everywhere: Italy, Singapore, the Philippines. Even England bought six episodes.

And the folks back home loved it. The response in Nashville affirmed that NBC was broadening the base for the peculiar blend of country music with rhythm and blues, Mandrell style. Barbara was ecstatic: "Now it's like you feel when you are in the school play—and it's the best one yet." It *was* the best one yet.

Director Bob Henry deftly utilized the talents of Barbara and her sisters. The typical format during its two-year run included music, dancing by the stars, a flow of big names and a standard closing gospel medley. Barbara's strong will was exerting its influence more and more, contrary to earlier days at the networks, when compromises eventually led to a watering down of her agenda.

Mary Mandrell, a slightly older version of her talented daughter, told reporter Lee Rector what the show meant to her: "My pride for these girls has nothing to do with the work. We have always been in music and I guess we're just used to that.

"Irlene helped Barbara out when she first started out with a band by playing with Barbara in her band. Now Barbara is helping Irlene. And they're such good girls. I just couldn't be happier for them."

Barbara commented, "Last year when we had our first show and they came in with the ratings and said it was number one for the time period, it was a very neat feeling because everyone told us variety shows were dead. I wanted to make sure I could make a country music show that would stay strong enough in the ratings to hold thirty or forty million people, but still keep my mainstream country fans.

"It seems like I should say the best thing I've gotten from the series is popularity, because I'm very grateful to have the chance to have new people that have never seen me before discover what I do."

Newspaper accounts put the feat somewhere near impossible. The star was, in effect, competing with herself. Each show got better, brighter. Each production number got a little more lavish. The combined effect continued to boost the ratings.

The strain was enormous, as Barbara threw all her creative energies into the production. She was involved in every detail, from costume changes to scripting. She particularly worried over the musical aspects, blocking dance numbers, choosing instrumentals and selecting show tunes.

She moved into previously untapped areas of her talent: interviews with guests and comedy sketches. And, of course, there was still the pure joy of her first love, singing.

But the pressure was unrelenting. Business negotiations did their share to drain away her energies, as did worrying over contracts and all the while keeping one eye open for her sisters, her husband and her kids.

It took its toll. Always being in control meant she worked sixteen-hour days, endured constant rehearsals and endless retakes. Barbara wanted perfection. The fight to attain it placed considerable strain on her and on the family. Eventually, it culminated in hospitalization for exhaustion.

And finally, she placed a strain on the one item that was the source of it all: her vocal chords. Consulting with her doctors, she made the decision to discontinue the series after the 1981–1982 season.

She explained that the decision had nothing to do with money. "My complaint was that I could not work the rigid schedule I did last season. Then I was involved in more than just performing. I was helping with the direction, the scripts, and some of the casting.

"I just knew that if I went through with another season as I did the first, it might result in a physical breakdown."

She was calling it quits at the peak of her game. She was leaving just as the public had had its appetite whetted for more. Leave 'em hanging. Make 'em want more. The decision showed her marketing savvy. Overexposure is always a danger. Get out before the market gets saturated. It was a calculated risk, but it just might work.

The decision was not casually made, however. Almost from the beginning, Barbara had had reservations about doing the show. Turning out quality entertainment week after week was a grind. She soon realized the quality was suffering. They fell into a rut. It was now down to working the formula. Play some music, do a little comedy, interview a guest. Sing your song, you're through. Go home and wait for the ratings.

Barbara never quite wanted it that way. She decided to hang it up while she was on top. But there was still the family to consider. Would the sisters drop off the edge of the world, never to be seen again?

The former child-star had emerged at the end of the series a hardened veteran of negotiations, of meetings with those who would try to make her career into something she might not want it to be, of pressure to give and give until you were all used up. She was tough, but TV was tougher. It made her want to get back on the road again.

She was undoubtedly at the peak of her career. As is not the case with some who drop out, Barbara's departure from television made her only more popular. Her fans increased, offers for movies and shows poured in. These were times to consider all the options.

"Yes, I have had some throat problems," she said. "Nothing serious, but the problem required a few treatments from a doctor. However, the doctor says the only thing my throat needs is rest. I believe him. I am still a little bit hoarse.

"NBC's bosses were very nice about my decision not to return next season. They understood that my throat was weary from wear. A weekly show is not an easy assignment. It's practically a full-time grind, constantly on your mind. We (NBC and I) have talked about some specials for 1982–1983. Sure, we'll proably do one or two—maybe more.

"It was one of the greatest experiences of my career as an entertainer. Everything associated with it—especially the response from viewers—was positive. I am thankful I got to do it.''

She immediately set about making plans for an extensive tour. ''I have been away from the fans for a long time, since last summer, and I'm looking forward to getting back out on the road.'' She wanted to get back to where it all began. It was like a cleansing, a rejuvenation. The TV industry had sucked all her energy out. The fans could put it all back. That is the way she approached the touring concept.

Barbara made plans for a three-and-one-half-month summer tour in 1982. She would also make another album. Before the summer began, however, two of her records had gone gold: *Barbara Mandrell Live* and *In Black and White*.

She also continued to rack up awards that attested to her popularity. In 1981, for the second time, she was named the Country Music Association's Entertainer of the Year. She was also named Female Vocalist of the Year by the same organization.

Music City News lauded her and her sisters with four of their top honors: Female Vocalist of the Year, Musician of the Year, Best Comedy Act, Best TV Series. Other magazines to recognize her again were *Billboard, Record World* and *Cashbox*. Her crowning achievement, however, was in the field of fashion. She concluded 1981 on one of the world's more pointless lists as one of Mr. Blackwell's Worst Dressed Women!

Before leaving her TV series in 1982, Barbara had also made her mark in viewers' eyes as a regular People's Choice Award winner for Favorite All-Around Female Entertainer, Favorite Female TV Personality and Favorite Female Musical Performer. *Music City News* also bestowed top honors once again. And the Tennessee Sports Hall of Fame named her distinguished Tennessean of the Year for her contribution to her home state.

Obviously there were many young performers watching her skyrocketing career, and she gave this advice to would-be singers in 1981: "This may not sound like earthshaking advice, but believe me, it really is S-O-L-I-D. I think aspiring young singers underestimate working for little vocal groups, or appearing at civic functions. That's what it is all about. It is working and getting well-known. The key word is experience.

"I was lucky and did a lot of things like that before I started recording. You can't learn to be a performer any-where else except on stage. Even if God gave you the natural ability, you have to develop it."

She continued: "And, of course, you must work very hard at it. But beyond that, one of those performances might lead to something bigger and better. You might meet somebody who could help you. Or you might be exposed to someone who has pull.

"The main ingredient, I think, in being successful is talent. That's the bottom line. An equal portion could be personality and attitude—something within you that will not let you settle for anything less than success."

Shortly after finishing the series, Barbara began working toward the realization of a project that had been on the drawing board for a long time. Gospel music had played an early role in the formation of Barbara's career. She had been moving toward making a gospel album for a long time. Now, with one obligation finished, she took up another.

Barbara collected popular Christian recording artists whose talents would be able to blend with her unique style. The

completed album, *He Set My Life to Music,* presented her
favorite songs of worship, traditional and contemporary.
Andrae Crouch, Dottie Rambo, the Blackwood Brothers
and B. J. Thomas joined with Barbara. On one song,
"Then, Now, and Forever," Barbara was backed up by
the Mt. Pisgah Gospel Chorus.

This album came as no surprise to a true fan. One need
only look at her background to understand the roots of her
music. Barbara began by singing in churches, and her
family has a deep gospel music heritage. She always mentions "the Lord" in her concerts. This surprises more
traditional keepers of the faith, for she does not bill herself
as a gospel singer and the content of some of her earlier
songs was not exactly church fare, though she always
managed to sing them in a way that sounded acceptable.
Yet, underneath, the fabric of traditional southern gospel
shows through.

Many thought that at this time in her life Barbara would
drop from the scene. Certainly, her popularity was over-
extended. She had won too much. She was too clean, too
goody-goody. People get tired of that. Critics said once the
series ended she would become a has-been.

Enter the amazing capability of the mass media. She
was etched in people's minds. They continued to buy her
albums. She commanded top dollar on the tour circuit.
Seats were always sold out at her concerts. Everywhere
one turned, her face appeared. She stared out at a persis-
tently adoring public from TV screens, women's magazines and supermarket tabloids. Television fan magazines
continued to follow her career, as did newspapers. She
seemed to be on every talk show and did endless charity
benefits. She had long since perfected her craft, but, compulsively, she continued to push herself to her absolute

limits. Yet the key to her continuing success was more than boundless energy, more even than media omnipresence. Her success continued, most of all, because she courted her fans.

3

Fans

FANS HAVE ALWAYS been an integral part of Barbara Mandrell's career and the principal source of her motivation. Her desire to please as well as promote her image has been embodied in her fans. She plans her shows around them. She plans her tours around them. She makes financial decisions based on what she thinks they would like. They are "the boss." If she were a publicly held corporation, the fans would be members of the board of directors and the majority stockholders. She knows they pay the bills.

Out of this concept, Barbara has developed the reputation of being immediately accessible to her fans. She signs autographs for hours. She hosts breakfasts for them each year. She goes out of her way to remember their names, to read their letters, even personally to write them little notes.

It's easy to become a Barbara Mandrell fan. All that's necessary is to send five dollars to her post office box in Hendersonville, Tennessee, then sit back and wait for a pastel-pink packet with its membership card, fan photo and fan newsletter.

The monthly newsletter gives her fans the most revealing glimpses of Barbara's day-to-day activities: her whereabouts, her vacation high jinks, reports on the children's progress and news of tour dates. She answers fan questions, reveals the names of her favorite singers, TV shows and personal tastes. The most intimate details of Barbara's life can be found in each sizzling issue, as well as "insider" photos.

She exudes charm and sincerity, capitalizing on her uncanny ability to make the audience feel that she cares. What she projects is genuineness. This is her greatest talent.

The fans sense this about her and they love it. Consider, for example, the 1987 Valentine's Day issue. She wrote it on white paper with lots of red ink and heart-shaped decorations. In it she revealed that she was planning to take a sleeping bag to Louise's house one night for a slumber party with her girlfriends. She admitted that it had been some time since she'd been to one, but remembered such parties fondly and was looking forward to the occasion. The planned activities were modest, by any standard. They intended to play Bingo and Yahtzee. Perhaps they would even sit up all night, "talking and giggling."

In ongoing fashion, Barbara also offers hints of her children's exploits in these newsletters, giving the reader the sense of being able to watch them grow. Her son Matt has been fooling around with the guitar, and Barbara expresses amazement at his apparent gift for the instrument. Matt wants formal training and, like any mother whose child shows an inclination to formal musical study, she reveals that she will be getting him a teacher for a while, on a trial basis, to make certain he is ready for the discipline before committing to a full-blown program. (This is from the same person who was playing several instruments by Matt's age. Since this leisurely approach seems inconsistent with her approach to her own career and development, it suggests that perhaps Barbara has geared down a little for the sake of her kids.)

Nothing is too inconsequential for discussion. In informing her fans about a haircut for Nathaniel, she also informs them that her father's brother, John Ira Mandrell, who is also a minister, used to be a barber. John Ira came in all the way from Arkansas to give Nathaniel his first haircut. It has special significance for both Barbara and Ken because her uncle had also given Matt his first haircut.

She takes a poll in a newsletter to see what kind of songs or styles the fans desire to see on her upcoming album. She has turned this into a trademark and it has paid off. The souvenir stand in the Barbara Mandrell Country Museum has almost anything one might possibly want to buy, always with her picture on it: books, records, trinkets, buttons. Her popular sisters are also included in the museum's offerings. The memorabilia are all there, too, for a price. It is, after all, the only place where one can obtain such collectibles.

When fans come in direct contact with her, they often don't know how to behave. Though approachable, she at the same time commands distance. Her effect is powerful, the aura unmistakable. She fills up the room. Her presence forces one to keep his distance. Paradoxically, her warmth creates a tension; one wants to go up to her and talk, make conversation, but the presence itself somehow intimidates.

Barbara's ability to read the crowd is uncanny. She sizes them up quickly. She gives them what they want, sometimes at the expense of what she wants, from hours of autographing to singing songs that really don't quite fit with her tastes.

This gift translates into all other facets of her career, into the lens of the camera, and into the microphone. She transcends the mechanisms and technology to cut straight to the heart.

The popular press verifies her regard for fans, and makes it clear that they are foremost in her priorities. The array is simple: God, country, family, fans. The fans are fixated on her and she is compulsively attentive to them.

Barbara's fans come in several varieties: the real, live "can't-wait-to-see-Barbara-perform" fan; the card-carrying, newsletter-toting "I was country when country wasn't cool" fan; the fan with a map of Opryland in one pocket and directions to Barbara's house on Henderson Lake in the other. But the differences are superficial. All Barbara Mandrell fans blend aspects of each type.

Theresa Smith, a college senior, is typical. She is a person who knows where she is going. She has goals. She plans to teach school after graduation. She is rational. She is quite normal in every way except one: She is passionately loyal to Barbara Mandrell and all she represents, a dyed-in-the-wool true believer in the work and life of the singer.

"It started with the TV show," says Theresa. "That was the only contact with her that I had. She just seemed to be the kind of person you would want to have as a friend. I started seeing magazine articles, and other information about her here and there."

It is obviously easier to have Barbara as a kind of mentor and role model if you are interested in the same things she is. At the core of the typical fan's relationship with her is country music. Theresa confides, "I play the piano and enjoy music. All kinds. I enjoy classical, gospel, country." Music is the thread woven into a relationship characterized by intermittent contact and distant adoration.

"I first saw her in a concert in 1982 in Chattanooga, Tennessee, in person. I was real excited. I went with my family, my folks and my sister. I didn't hear about it until after the tickets had gone on sale. We were way up in the balcony with binoculars. We were trying to see this tiny little person way down on the stage.

"At that time, she would always sign autographs after her show. She would have a two-to-three-to-four-hour autographing session after her shows. That particular night, she was on her way to New Orleans, and there was some bad flooding. So she didn't get to stay and sign. I was really disappointed. I was crushed because I wasn't going to get to meet her."

What does the young college student recall best? "Her *energy*. She made the whole audience come alive. She's very energetic, vivacious. She puts a lot into it. She works hard at it. She makes you feel like you got your money's worth. Very entertaining. The music. Going from instrument to instrument. Very proficient on each instrument she used."

Even fandom as passionate as Theresa's is not totally devoid of self-awareness, however. It is as if a part of her identity is created by or feeds on the awareness of *being* a fan. Theresa bears this out when she says, "She has a unique rapport with the audience. Laughing, talking, just making you feel at ease with her. People were constantly bringing things to the stage: roses, flowers, balloons. She was very personal—relating well to them. You didn't get bored at all. She was always cracking jokes, good sense of humor, but could also show a sincere side. Very compassionate."

Could Barbara turn on the juice? Theresa remembered the star's performance. "She was electric. It made you just want to stand up and yell. My dad just stood up and whistled and hollered. He really got into it. Old people, young people, no age barriers."

She continued: "Her band impressed me. They were very clean-cut. Very polished. Professional. They had a good relationship and rapport with her and she with them. They were all very talented on their own instruments. Just a very polished act."

Of course, a Barbara Mandrell fan would never miss an opportunity to see Barbara. If concerts weren't enough, there were other opportunities for contact. Two months after the concert she described, Theresa went to the annual breakfast held especially for Barbara's fans. She had been very sick and feared that unless she improved, her parents would not let her go.

"I was going to it if I had to go on a stretcher! I didn't care. About three days before, I was sick and felt clammy. I went around the house ha-ha-ing, trying to act OK. I faked 'em out.

"When I got there, I was really hyper. I had my camera, my tape recorder, the whole bit. It was the Opryland Hotel, in the Presidential Ballroom, a sit-down breakfast. Barbara's husband said a prayer at the beginning. Bobby Jones and the New Life Singers sang some songs. There were games, like a take-off of game shows. People came out of the audience. Everyone was involved. They had prizes for the oldest member there. I estimate several thousand people. It was huge. Even with that many people, you still felt like she was interacting with you.

"*Good Morning America* was there. It lasted a couple of hours. Then she had an autographing session that lasted three or four hours. I stood in line for four and a half hours. She signed the entire time, always with a smile, always with a kind word, always allowing you to have your picture made with her. Never acting tired. Just very relaxed and talkative.

"I was so excited. This was the first time I had met her. I thought my heart was going to come out of my chest. I got up to her. I don't even remember what I said. But she just put you so at ease immediately. There's nothing to be nervous about.

"I've seen people at concerts go up on stage, cry, forget their names. There's one part of her act where she plays the harmonica. She usually gets someone from the audience to come up on stage and play it with her. One girl got up there and just burst into tears, she was so excited to meet Barbara. She was just sobbing. Barbara put the microphone down and put her arms around her. She just stood there beside her and talked to her for a few minutes. After that the girl was fine, she calmed down.

"She has a basic road show that follows the same format. Like maybe the song she has out that year. For example, her favorite song is 'Battle Hymn of the Republic.' The first concert I went to, she sang that. At the second chorus, they modulated and dropped the flag down from the ceiling. It just sent cold chills all over you. She has such a powerful voice with that song. . . ."

Theresa shares her insights into Barbara's career as a recording artist: "I have all the albums. All the tapes. From the first one to the last. Progressively better. [The first one is] more country. She's more polished now. You can tell just from the sound of her voice that she was younger and less experienced. The last one is called *Moments*. It's digitally recorded. It's fantastic. It has some country, a couple of blues—she loves blues—and does it very well. The title cut is a beautiful love song, perfect for any wedding. It ranges from country to blues, to more pop. . . .

"I have actually met her face to face maybe fifteen times. I also go to a benefit she has every year in the fall in Birmingham, Alabama. It's open to the public. It's called the Sheriff's Boys' and Girls' Ranches there in Birmingham. These are homes for kids that are abandoned or abused. She has a benefit that includes a golf and tennis tournament. She usually does a concert. She didn't do one last year, or the year after the accident. But usually there is one. All the proceeds go to these homes. They receive tens of thousands of dollars that go directly to the benefit.

"This is where I first got a chance to have a conversation with her. It was at a celebrity tennis tournament in 1983. I went with a friend from college. We were in a parking lot outside where the match was. Everyone was just standing around watching.

"Barbara came out and I remember she had on white pants and a turquoise knit shirt and turquoise tennis shoes. Just casual—sunglasses and a purse. Just real, real casual. She was by herself.

"I bought a sponsorship. I could have played golf, I could have played tennis, but I'm not a pro, I just went to watch."

Reliving the encounter with her goddess, Theresa becomes extremely animated: "I was sitting on the bumper of a car with my friend. Barbara sat down about two cars away on another car bumper. She was just sitting there. My friend, Sara, said, 'Go over there and talk to her.' I said, 'No, I'm not going to go over there and talk to her.' She said, 'Well, just go over there and say hello to her.'

"We kind of argued back and forth. I kept saying 'No' and she kept saying 'Yes' and finally I got up the gumption to go over there and talk to her. And I introduced myself and she said, 'Well, have a seat.' I just sat down on the bumper of the car, and we just talked.

"I remember when she was getting ready to go—I believe it was a People's Choice Awards show and she was telling me that she was really nervous about it and she had butterflies and she wished it was over with. We just talked about things I was taking at school and a guy I was dating. She asked me different questions about my major and what school I went to and where it was, what I planned to do when I graduated, and personal questions like that.

"She told me what she had been doing for the last while. Just very informal conversation, small talk. We probably talked thirty-five, maybe forty minutes, just sitting there.

"That's when I really got to see Barbara the person, not Barbara the entertainer. Very warm. Very sincere. Genuine. Very genuine, not fake at all. Very loving. Considerate. She seemed interested. It wasn't like, 'Get away from me, I want to be by myself.' It wasn't like that at all. Just very warm. I was very impressed. She lets you see, 'Hey, I'm not a superstar, I'm just a human being like everybody else.' And that is when I quit thinking of her as Barbara Mandrell the Superstar and just started thinking of her as Barbara Mandrell the person. And I have ever since."

Theresa, living a charmed life as far as fans go, managed to meet Mandrell on several occasions. Each time, her admiration grew stronger. "She hasn't had as many concerts since her accident. The first tour back after the accident—it was called the 'Get to the Heart' tour—we went to five concerts on that tour. . . .

"I've met her husband and all three of her children. Ken, her husband, has a great sense of humor. He always has something going. That's what stands out about him.

They seem to get along very well. He seems to be very considerate of her and she of him.''

Theresa, like all true fans, has visited the Mecca of the total Barbara Mandrell experience, the Barbara Mandrell Country Museum. "I've been probably five or six times. Very impressive. I think it would be enjoyable to anyone, not just a Barbara fan or a country music fan. I know everyone doesn't feel the way I do about Barbara Mandrell. I'd be stupid to think that. I think that anyone who does would have to appreciate her, to feel a little something for her, just from going through.

"It's very personal. There are videos. There are home movies. There's everything from her wedding dress to all of her awards. She remade the nursery for one of her children, her daughter. She painted a mural on the wall herself. Very impressive and very interesting.

"She has a gift shop. It's not just Barbara Mandrell stuff in the gift shop. There's all kinds of little gifts. It's not like it's just pushing Barbara Mandrell off on the public. It's very informative, and set up in the way that you can see things close up. You can go at your pace. Very neat.''

Theresa was devastated by the news of Mandrell's wreck in 1984. She felt as if it had happened to a member of her own family. She kept every clipping and scrap of information printed about it.

"[Barbara] is a little more serious now. I wouldn't say she is a person who doesn't laugh. When I say serious I guess [I mean] more aware of life. Not taking life so lightheartedly. Being thankful for today.

"In fact, I remember a press conference she held—while she was still on crutches, just a few months after the accident. She said one of the things she had learned was that 'we're not promised tomorrow, just today.' She seems closer to her family, and she was always very family oriented.

"She is not as driven as before. She was one of these people who would push themselves absolutely to the limit in her work. Now, her family time is more important to her, which I think is good.

"I've seen her since then, and have talked with her. I've seen her at a couple of concerts. She remembered me. I've seen her at two breakfasts and a benefit since the accident. As a matter of fact, I saw her at the breakfast after [the wreck]. This really got me. It was in 1985, in June.

"She was big-as-a-barrel-pregnant, still having problems getting around with her broken ankle. And yet, she signed autograph after autograph in the blazing heat outside. It was big-time hot. This was in the parking lot at Barbara Mandrell Country, after the breakfast after she had already signed two or three hours.

"She hasn't had the kind of autographing sessions she used to, due to her health. And she has a new baby. That takes up time and that I can understand.

"As far as still being personal with her fans, she is. I've been to concerts before where an entertainer was like, 'Don't touch me.' Maybe throw out his hand, get a grasp of his fingers. She's not like that at all. She's still as warm, as giving, as loving. She just doesn't put as much demands on her time as she did before."

For Theresa, and for most dedicated fans, keeping up with Barbara Mandrell is an obsession. Predictably, the chief by-product of this process is a scrapbook with clippings and stories that have been scoured from every possible source. Theresa is proud of her own treasured collection of memorabilia.

"Gosh, I have two big photo albums that are packed full. I let her see them one time. I saw her in Michigan one week and was going to see her in Knoxville, Tennessee, the next.''

Chasing after Barbara has taken Theresa on twelve-hour jaunts to tour dates. From Michigan to Jacksonville, Florida, this fan is relentless.

''She was shocked to see me there in Michigan. We ended up by chance with fourth-row seats. We were supposed to be way in the balcony and somebody canceled and we got their tickets. My roommate and I made this sign that read HELLO BARBARA, FROM CHARLESTON, TENNESSEE. She looked at the sign. The lights were in her eyes. She said, 'I see who that is.' Then she said, 'Girl, what are you doing here?'

''I said, 'I came up to Michigan to see this concert.' She said, 'You're kiddin'.' I said, 'Naw, really, we came up to see the concert.' This banter was going on in front of thousands of other ticket holders.

''She said, 'Can I have that sign?' Then she said, 'Well, bring it up here.' So I got up and took it to her up on stage. She put the microphone down and she looked at me with this funny look and said, 'Now tell me, what are you really doing in Michigan?'

''I said, 'I really came to see the concert.' She just couldn't believe it. We talked about three or four minutes just standing there. She bent down and kissed my cheek. I didn't know it, but I had lipstick on my cheek.

''At the end of the concert, she called my roommate and me back up to the stage and she gave each of us one of her drummer's drumsticks which have BARBARA MANDRELL SHOW—MCA RECORDS written on them.

''I gave her the scrapbooks then. She kept them for a week and then brought them back to me in Knoxville the next. She had already autographed one of them. Then she autographed the other one.

"I have two shelves full of material that I haven't had the time to put into scrapbooks. So if I had it all together, I'd probably have about five or six huge albums full of stuff."

Predictably, Theresa is a devout Christian. Barbara is too. It's a big part of her appeal to much of her following. Wholesomeness counts, but by all accounts it is the fact that Barbara is a believer herself that is central to the largest part of her fanatical following. Theresa is reluctant to judge Barbara's faith. Some fundamentalist Christians have been skeptical because she doesn't conform to the stereotypical image of one who claims to be born-again. But Theresa is convinced. "I don't feel like we can ever be sure about anyone but yourself. But you can have a good idea. You can feel. I feel that she is a devout Christian.

"At the first benefit I went to, they had a big ditty bag that had all kinds of things from different sponsors. As a gift to the people who bought the sponsorships, she had a Bible inside a cedar chest. Really nice.

"Her favorite Bible verse is Romans 8:28. I had cross-stitched a picture that had that Bible verse on it and had given it to her. I had her sign my Bible. She put her name and my name in it, and the date. She handed it back to me and then she said, 'Wait just a minute, I forgot something.' She looked at me and winked and she wrote Romans 8:28. That really touched me.

"Never does a concert go by that she doesn't mention the Lord. She's very up front about her feelings. She'll tell you she's raised Pentecostal. They were called 'pew-jumpers.' She is very up front, very sincere about her relationship with God. She's not ashamed of it. She's not embarrassed about it. She just tells you the way she feels."

What attracts a superfan like Theresa to Barbara instead of someone else in the entertainment galaxy?

"The talent was the initial thing. And then just her personality. When you meet Barbara Mandrell, you feel she really cares. She always makes you feel welcome. She is appreciative of any little thing you do for her.

"She genuinely is a Christian, which is important to me. That draws me to her. I have never seen anyone who could pour out love just the way she does. She keeps giving it. You can feel it."

Obviously, not all fans are like Theresa Smith, though there are thousands of others who are. They count among their ranks other entertainers, people Barbara has toured with, those who have been on her show, singers she has performed with. There are many. To be an entertainer's entertainer takes quite a knack.

Queen Barbara is at the height of her reign. This becomes apparent when an attempt is made to get through to her offices. Her publicist guards her schedule like an MP. Even getting Jeannie Ghent, who is the closest thing to a Hydra with a southern drawl and who controls access to Barbara, on the line to talk about talking about Barbara is an ordeal.

At some point, the thought arises: Is Mandrell's accessibility an illusion? Is all this business of being there for her followers just a facade? Is it part of the act?

Since 1984, she has seemed less enthusiastic about her career in general. The tragedy has taken its toll, and the changes have spilled over into the total image package the general public seems to devour.

The trademark characteristic of accessibility is much like Dolly Parton's wigs. Barbara puts it on and pulls it off. It is part of the costume.

As a wealthy public figure she is vulnerable. There are crazies and terrorists out there. There are bloodsuckers who would latch on to someone of Barbara's stature if she didn't have some barriers to keep them away. The Mandrell organization is a tight-knit community. While fostering an image of openness, the palace guard constantly works to isolate the Queen. Interviews are guarded. Media coverage is well planned, even manipulated. The press is used to the Queen's advantage.

It is argued that the rights of her family do not warrant the disclosure of any details about her private life. The problem is that the illusion of intimacy is exactly what she has built the foundation on. She can go only so far to please everybody. There will be some neurotics who always want more.

The public's demands are overwhelming. In our society, the press regards itself as the one institution with the right to violate the sanctity of the home. The family life Barbara Mandrell has built is not for public consumption. It is far different stuff than her entertainment. It is not a commodity that is to be used up and thrown away. It is not a music selection that fades after the last tremolo dies.

There are other people to consider—her family, her staff. True, their lives are affected by the career of the entertainer. They are a part of her experience. By default, they become a part of the fans' domain when she includes them as part of the act.

This then becomes her special dilemma. To what extent does someone of Barbara Mandrell's stature draw the line? Where does she stop? She can't have it both ways.

The whole structure of her life requires a delicate balance. In marketing herself, she must choose between personal privacy and a loyal following who insist on having an inside track to the performer and her family. They exact a high price.

4

Touring

HOME AWAY FROM home is the Prevost bus. It sleeps nine in bunk-style beds. There is a modest bedroom privately partitioned for the diminutive entertainer. There is the usual assortment of gadgets: television, microwave, refrigerator, sofa, dinette. But by industry standards, the whole affair is still rather modest.

Barbara has traveled in one fashion or another since she was twelve. At the same time, she has managed as a mother and a wife while simultaneously pursuing a career on the highway.

Road groups in the music industry have not had the best of reputations. Yet for Barbara, touring is as different from the usual industry practice as is every other facet of her empire. She has always managed to pull things off in such a way as to make them look desirable, respectable. It is her trademark and it even applies to traveling on the road with her band.

This aspect of the musician's lifestyle is the great killer.

It is something akin to joining the circus, which is every parent's worst nightmare. A road musician faces many difficulties and is continually confronted with seductive opportunities that can make him wind up on the skids.

Touring is a drain on both physical and mental resources. Traveling, singing your way from place to place, never sleeping in the same town three nights in a row—it's tough enough for a single musician, and even tougher for someone married, with a family. Tours and road work are the single most prominent cause of marital break-up among entertainers. Mandrell seems to have found a way to manage; she calls it "turning adversity into an asset."

Willie Nelson produced a movie about the road. Countless songs refer to the strain and stress it exacts. The folklore is replete with images of the lifestyle the road breeds and with tales of alcohol, substance abuse and illicit sexual trysts. These stories are all too common among devotees of country and western groups. They are the fabric of the subculture.

Travel also presents physical strains: constant exposure to new environments, having to adapt to an endless stream of strange new faces, the stresses imposed by loneliness and illness. The road musician is always giving and giving. The quality of the music suffers in time. Life on the bus is complicated and interesting, but it is always difficult—and sometimes impossible—to find privacy.

The group either is family, becomes like family or eventually bites the dust. Back home, the real family, or what's left of it, waits by the door. The wanderer comes home occasionally to dry out, to wait for the next gig, tank up, then head back out on the road.

Since Barbara travels three weeks out of every month, early on she tried, especially on long trips away from home, to take Matt with her. To the present, she has continued this tradition with all three of her children.

The family act is an extension of her family life. She and her dad do a little comedy. He kids her just as he would at home. For instance, she sometimes wears a purple jumpsuit and when he first sees her he does a double-take and says, "She looks like a ninety-pound grape."

Since she spends so much of her time on the bus, she has learned to use it well. She catches up on her sleep, answers fan mail and at one time she even did her own hair. Lately, though, Barbara has evidently had second thoughts about the wisdom of such a practice. She has acquired the services of a hairdresser as well as someone to help with the kids.

She believes the effort is worth it. Barbara loves to entertain live audiences, and does not see herself as just a singer. Her concept of her role is larger: She's an entertainer.

Barbara also loves to meet her fans individually. Sometimes she's the only one in the show who will come out afterward and sign autographs. She has admitted that she occasionally feels awkward coming out by herself, but her devotion to her fans doesn't let her feel that way long. She is particularly happy to meet children, and loves it when some little boy asks for a hug.

She finds post-show decompression to be the most difficult aspect of touring. She gets excited, even keyed up, doing her act. Afterward, when she's got to come down, she often feels the need to sit down by herself, drink a Coke and rest for a few minutes.

Barbara has been quoted as saying, "When we travel, my family, and my band, we're tame. Nothing wild ever goes on in this bus! I won't even let my band members wear blue jeans while we travel because you can't tell a nice pair from a ratty pair.''

Her concern for image goes even further. When the band leaves the bus to eat at truckstops, she wants them to look like true professionals. She doesn't allow drinking of any sort when on tour. She frowns on even as little as one glass of beer before a concert. She works on the assumption that if a fan smells beer on your breath, as far as he's concerned, you're drunk. She is acutely aware that musicians have a bad image to overcome as it is. Nor will she let the band smoke on stage, even in the wings. She feels that nothing looks worse than someone on stage or waiting in the wings smoking a cigarette.

Over the years Barbara has developed another set of concerns—those of a parent on the road, dealing with the conflicting demands of family obligations and the constant traveling that has been the backbone of her popular career. After a tour one summer with the family, the kids were getting ready to go back to school and Barbara lamented to one interviewer, ''I'm going through a very traumatic time. Jaime will leave me next week; Ken will be coming to get her because school starts. It will be my first time on the road without a baby and it's killing me. The kids and the bus—those are the two things that let me be sort of a normal person in a very abnormal existence. My eating habits and my sleep can be okay on the bus. And if it weren't for the bus, I couldn't have the kids with me. I certainly couldn't drag them through the airports at all hours of the night. Jaime can be bathed and in bed by the time I'm finished with the show. Or, if we don't want to go to bed, we can read, play games or watch a movie.''

Even for ordinary people, raising children and being married are not easy. A woman like Barbara, whose career is so all-consuming that she's never away from it, has to work extra hard just to make her schedule work. For instance, on one occasion she had two travel days between concerts in northern California and Chicago, so she flew home with the children to take them to buy new school clothes. She knew she wasn't going to get another chance for a long while, and that kind of intimate family activity is something she likes to do herself.

Some time ago Barbara told a questioner, "You can always make do. We've been through a lot of earaches on the road with my son. One time, however, it was the worst and I didn't have anything to treat him. His fever was going up and I couldn't get it down. I called my pediatrician from a twenty-four-hour drugstore in Wyoming and he told me what to get. You can do it. It just takes a little effort to handle all of it."

What about children raised in a bus? Would they be able to function socially? She told one reporter that "the compliments I receive about both my children are just phenomenal. And it means everything to me. Because whatever else I do, if I neglect the rearing of my children, it doesn't mean a darn thing.

"God entrusts our children to us and we have to do it the best way we know how. I do not judge other people, but for me, I prefer children that are respectful. It hurts me to see a child sass an adult or talk back. When I was seventeen, it was very popular to say 'So?' Well, one time my father said something to me—I don't even remember what it was—and I said, 'So?' and I got the back of his hand across my face. I deserved it because I was being disrespectful to my father. That's why I love my father and mother so much and respect them. They deserve and earned my respect; they demanded it and I try to do the same with my children."

Just an old-fashioned girl, Barbara carries on the family traditions from the back of a bus on the road to anywhere.

The road gets in the blood. It's a mutant virus, a life form peculiar to the twentieth century. Ninety percent of the touring musician's time is spent going to or coming from a gig while just a very short time is used to set up and deliver the goods, to do what he came to do. Then it's back out on the road again to somewhere new.

Every venue, from small theater to giant arena, presents its own set of peculiar problems. Each new stage has to be sized up. The acoustic qualities have to be evaluated, then the massive assortment of technology from the cavernous underbelly of the bus must be hauled out. The pieces have to be assembled in such a way as to provide consistency with the night before, in spite of the fact that all the acoustical properties and physical aspects of the new location are probably completely different from anything else they have seen. The amps and the layout from where they operate are about the only things that don't change from day to day. But the only major thing that is constant is the on-stage act. It is the one piece of security a musician has.

In spite of the challenges, the road is highly addictive. It's risky. The thrill of going into a new location and creating the same responses time after time becomes the prize. This is the heartthrob of performers. With evangelistic fervor they continue the quest. A well-executed show, against heavy odds, provides a sense of aesthetic accomplishment. This pride is elusive and difficult for the non-musician to understand. But it is the kind of experience that lures the performer, star and unknown alike, back to the road time and time again.

Unfortunately, there is another driving force behind all this. A deeper drawing power pushes those who go out there to the land of one-night stands. It is a capitalistic phenomenon. It is called marketing. But what it really means is big business.

The greatest album ever produced sells only if the people can hear it. They will respond even better if they can catch the performance live, in person. The lights and the glamor entice the fans, but there is an ulterior purpose to the live appearance, one the fans are seldom moved to think about: the bottom-line potential. The music business is money-driven. As a consequence, many performers get yoked into a tour schedule that becomes tiresome, imprisoned in a configuration created by higher management.

The pressure is great. The creative mix is complex: high-quality talent, a cohesive band, an innovative producer, a top-of-the-line studio. The business side is less glamorous, but probably more important: It consists of record distributors, concert promoters, artists, costume designers. A touring show exists to generate record sales, and putting a tour together demands a small army. Cash to foot the bills comes from a backer, a sponsor; an aggressive agent arranges the gigs; a support team takes care of the details. But none of it works unless the musician can draw on a large pool of fans willing to go some distance to catch the concert.

Equipment, technical expertise, innovative programming, transportation, logistics—all these sound like terms from a course in military tactics at West Point. In effect, they might as well be. On some level, the problems are identical. How do you get from here to there in the best time, making sure you have everything you need once you arrive? That has always been an army's primary concern. And the small armies of musicians and roadies who crisscross the country on a daily basis, striking like cultural guerrillas then moving on, are not that different. They constitute a whole sublevel of the business, with enormous profits at stake. Instead of a piece of territory, they are looking to conquer a share of the market.

And here's where Mandrell shines. This is the substance at the core of it all: good business management combined with a family cohesiveness. Just as ancient soldiers brought their families from place to place and battle to battle, armies moving like mobile cities across the countryside, Barbara has achieved her success by integrating family with business rather than separating one from the other. They move together.

This approach undeniably presents a set of unusual challenges. Doing it with a family on board requires balance. It demands something unique from the entire entourage. The support staff must maintain and agree with the standard, or at least not openly violate the code. Mandrell again has perfected the image and the concept.

Fans, at least, feel the squeaky-clean image transcends the stage and cuts through to the soul. Absent from this organization is self-destructive behavior. This is a family endeavor. It is a fresh concept, a rarity on the musical scene.

If the image is on the cutting edge, so is the product. Barbara's records not only stack up in quantity but also climb from good to better. Perfection is her obsession. She acts as if she invented it, and it has its price. She has changed producers several times in her career. She has sued her record company. She has had disagreements with the people in her orbit. Still, the quality goes up, the popularity quotient stays high.

Barbara was one of the first in Music City to get involved in digital recording. This state-of-the-art technique is the body and soul of the compact-disc process. The older, conventional method involved recording sound in analog form, that is, in sound waves that were an approximation of the real thing. Compact discs offer the highest quality sound recordings currently available.

The goal of the tour process is not just to sell records; there are other considerations. New material and new stage and lighting effects are tried out and honed to perfection. The constant, rapid evolution of musical technology means that new equipment must be road-tested. The tour can be a kind of traveling laboratory experiment, designed to discover what will work with the crowd—and what won't (that is something you have to learn quickly). Selling yourself and selling your stuff—T-shirts, buttons, bumper stickers, albums, tapes and CDs—is also part of touring, and it's grueling, backbreaking work.

The Mandrell energy makes her a prize commodity. People try to buy this at the end of the show. It's what they come for. This puts the heat on her to perform. She may not be feeling well. She might be tired. She might have a headache or a lot on her mind. It doesn't matter. The fans have shelled out for more than tickets. She's got to give it to them.

And give it to them she does, over and over and at consistently high levels. She steps out and does it, regardless of how she feels. She explodes with raw enthusiasm, naked energy. The fans get their money's worth.

The Do-Rites are no less energetic. They work extremely hard to keep up with their boss. She once described a trip with them, early in the road-show business, when things were still tight financially. Killing time on the bus, the band members had been discussing various jobs they'd held outside the music business. Barbara later said she felt left out because she'd never done anything to make a living but play music.

Barbara does not seem to feel restricted by not knowing

how to do anything but entertain. She freely admits that it would require a certain amount of training for her to pursue some other kind of work should that become necessary or even desirable, but she is confident she could learn to do it.

Most of us go through our entire lives without ever knowing our full capabilities, usually because of limited opportunity. Barbara, too, is uncertain about what she might do if music were no longer possible for her. In that respect, at least, she is no different from the rest of us.

Despite the rigors of touring, on more than one occasion Barbara has expressed her fondness for her taxing career. She is realistic enough to understand that if she were not a successful singer, her current lifestyle would be beyond her reach, but too often, she thinks, people are overly concerned with material possessions.

Not that she would prefer to do without her success and the things it has brought her—she adores oil paintings, furs, diamonds and Rolls-Royces—but she insists she could be happy without the kind of money her career has made possible.

It is interesting to examine her current attitude about the Do-Rites. In a 1983 interview with Neil Pond, editor of *Music City News,* she stated, "They're entertainers in their own right. They don't just stand there and pick and grin. . . . We not only work together, we live together, probably as much as any husband and wife do."

The incessant traveling also has its advantages. Unlike most country girls, Barbara has had the opportunity to travel all over the world.

On a recent trip to Saudi Arabia, she found it somewhat awkward to be a star in the Middle East. Upon her return, she recounted her difficulties to a Nashville-based magazine. The culture shock, unavoidable for a Westerner having her first exposure to an Islamic society, was considerable, and the work was every bit as grueling as it would have been in more familiar surroundings.

Ever solicitous of the art form that has made her wealthy, Barbara wanted her shows to be especially good because it was the first time country music had come to Saudi Arabia. She felt more country musicians might be invited to Saudi Arabia in the wake of her shows. As a result, she tried to conform as much as possible to Islamic customs, wearing long-sleeved shirts and sweaters and jackets, despite the heat.

Touring is something that has gotten into her blood. This was apparent at a news conference on Tuesday, February 4, 1986, as she revealed her plans to return to the touring circuit for the first time since the accident. "This is a real special day for me: I get to announce that I'm going to tour again. I am just elated and thrilled about it."

Her excitement about going back on the road was obvious. She was asked who would be with her. She replied, "The Marlboro people asked me who I wanted. It didn't take me long to think about it. I knew I was asking for the moon, but she's always been a special, dear friend to me." Of course, she was referring to Dolly Parton, who went along.

Barbara admitted that she would be physically limited by her injured ankle, but felt she would be able to move as much as her revamped show required. She wasn't up to playing softball or tennis, but the revised act took her condition into account.

Touring seems to be a therapy of sorts for Mandrell. On those rare occasions when she's been ill, the audience seems to stimulate her. Once she gets up on stage and the spotlight goes on, the adrenaline starts flowing and everything's fine. The audience is her perfect medicine. But, it is indisputable that performing on the road after the accident has presented her with a very special challenge.

The rigorous work schedule of touring musicians makes extraordinary demands on their physical stamina. Entertainers probably should take extra precautions with their health, but they never do. Barbara will admit that she doesn't eat wisely. If there's something else to do, she often doesn't even take the time to eat. On the bus, she usually just has cereal for breakfast and possibly a light lunch in the afternoon.

Since her show is physically demanding, she can't gorge herself and still give the type of performance she strives for. She will usually wait until after the show for a substantial meal. Since she stays around to sign autographs, that may not be until well after midnight. At that hour, in most parts of the country, the only places to get food are truck-stops or hamburger joints. So the evening meals are long on grease and short on nutrition.

Most entertainers find the road very tiring, but Barbara actually gets more sleep on the road than at home. She often can nap all day on the bus. She has even joked that she goes on the road to rest up.

It is obvious that Mandrell takes her responsibilities to her audience seriously. At the same time, she seemed somewhat defensive when a reporter asked her about the forced cancellations after her accident. "My career has been built on a tremendously solid foundation," said Barbara. "And that's why, when my shows had to be canceled, all the promoters had to tell people was, she's sick and in the hospital, and the fans would understand because we have a reliable reputation."

This same defensiveness has been provoked by discussions of her recording career. A few years ago, she reacted this way: "We've worked very, very hard at it. Now after it's all said and done, I'm glad my first records weren't overnight successes. I'm not in the business to get what I can and get out; I'm in it until it's time for me to retire. Every record I release sells more and more; again it's that gradual building, building, building. But something always seems to get in the way to keep them from becoming Number 1 hits.

"Like 'Woman to Woman'—it's been a tremendous success, with vast appeal. But when it came out, there was another record that was selling really well and hanging on to the Number 1 position. The same thing happened with 'Married but Not to Each Other.' I couldn't have asked for better records, quality-wise. So maybe it's just a question of luck."

Before the days of her own TV series, she had commented, "I've been fortunate to get on a lot of very good TV shows, and it was really a thrill for me to get the Grammy nomination for 'After the Lovin',' which was taken from one of my albums. I knew I probably wouldn't win, but it was still quite an honor."

But despite the glamor associated with the road, and the undeniable importance it has in maintaining a successful career, something in Barbara Mandrell would be just as happy staying at home. It often surfaces in interviews. "I like being home. Last night we grilled hamburgers and ate out here, and I felt like I was on vacation. All the cards and letters from fans have made me feel wonderful, too. I knew they all loved and cared but when I got sick it made me realize how much! My mother got a big kick out of me because every time some flowers would arrive I'd get so excited. At one time there were sixty to seventy bouquets in my room. I gave some away to people who didn't have any, but I kept most of them because they meant so much to me!"

And one of the genuine highlights of her career had come locally. HBO had taped her special, *The Lady Is a Champ,* at home in Tennessee. It was a Las Vegas-type review, and the name of her show became a nickname. The perky singer was very talkative about the show. She told Bob Millard in a *Nashville Banner* interview, published on July 12, 1983: "I received calls all day from friends of mine who said they couldn't get tickets because it sold out so fast. . . . I'm kind of glad because it's going to be the last time we do this show and I'm going to miss it."

Barbara was keeping her eye on the future as well. She had been studying Las Vegas shows while putting this one together. In another interview, she stated in regard to the show, "I wouldn't be able to do what I do if not for songwriters. The creative people I most admire are songwriters, authors, journalists—people who can put words together."

She believes hit records depend on people behind the scenes, many of whom are never known to the public. The artist is important, of course, and the most visible, but composers, engineers, producers and studio musicians also play a major role in the creation of a successful recording.

If a record gets help from a dozen people, a big show needs an army. This one had Barbara and her guests in no fewer than fifty-seven costumes. The behind-the-scenes people included sound technicians, lighting people, hair, makeup and costume people and stagehands to insure a smoothly run presentation.

Anticipation ran high, and Barbara was inundated with ticket requests from friends and strangers alike. That was to be expected, and it was not unusual. Show business seems to feed on itself, and its professionals make it a habit to stay in touch with one another. But when you bring a big operation home, and it's a neighbor, or the cousin of the grocery clerk, who wants a little help, the obligation takes on an unusually personal flavor.

For Barbara, the success of the show was a dream come true because she had wanted for two years to perform for the hometown crowd. Everyone in her organization wanted to be accepted by the people who mean the most—friends and neighbors.

It was a complicated process, and took months of preparation. Everything—from mulling over budgets and working out the complicated logistics of hauling in the huge sets to arranging for the dancers, the costumes, the hairstyles and all the rest of the production elements—was overwhelming.

But Barbara had another reason for doing the show. After the Nashville performance, the production was slated to be discarded. Her concern for freshness won't allow her to do the same old show year in and year out. She feels her fans expect something new and as a performer she feels obligated to deliver.

She planned to present a full package, determined that when the curtain went up, the audience wouldn't even be aware that it was witnessing a taping. The show was going to be taped in Nashville and edited in Los Angeles. For two days after the final edit, she'd be back home, only to leave immediately for Las Vegas with her new concert show.

In the new show, she intended to do just about everything she knew how to do . . . short of skiing. She had gone to Vegas on several different occasions to do homework two or three days at a time. If she was there for three days, she would watch six "star" shows to see what elements they all used. When it came time to put her own show together, she spent six weeks studying the preliminary plan. Then her adviser, Scott Salmon, went out on the road with her and they worked it out on the bus.

She recounted some of her anxieties to the *Banner* on July 29, 1983. Bob Millard got the story: "They told me when we got here that occupancy at the hotels on the strip was only 30 percent, but we played to a full house last night.

"I knew what I wanted to do, but I didn't know how to get it done. For instance, it really bothers me when someone [on stage] says, 'Excuse me while I go change clothes.' I just wanted it to have more surprise than that, and that made staging it all more difficult. There's one particular spot in the show where I've got 19–20 seconds to make a costume change. Those are tough. It doesn't sound so bad just talking about it, but doing it is just chaos. Therefore, even the wardrobe changes are choreographed. You work it out with the dresser, down to which leg goes in first . . . everything . . . I told someone earlier that I thought it took two semis to haul the sets for this show. But I was wrong—it takes four."

When it was all over, Barbara was elated at the results. It had been worth the effort. "I was really overwhelmed. I really expected a more conservative reception because there were so many industry people here and we tend to be jaded after a while. More than anything it was the facial expressions of the audience. They were so genuine and having such a good time. A couple of times up there I got all choked up. It was everything I wanted it to be and more."

Torn between the demands of her career and the reasonable, intelligent desire to lead a more stable, less unruly life, Mandrell has tried to walk the fine line between necessity and excess. While her heart is certainly in her music, at least a part of her would prefer a more sedentary existence, one that allowed her a more tranquil family life, far from the rigors of the road. Music-business realities being what they are, however, it is doubtful whether she will realize that ambition anytime soon.

5

Crisis

THE EVENTS LEADING up to September 11, 1984, were ordinary enough. Just another mom getting her kids ready for the start of another school year. The wreck itself was also commonplace in the sense that things like this happen every day to ordinary people. When a person of immense popularity is involved, though, it suddenly becomes a sensation.

This is the price Barbara pays for her fame. She can't just lie in a hospital, recuperating. Instead, the fans, the press and the public at large want to play a part. She has been there for so many people, as Louise put it, and now they wanted to be there for her.

Barbara's family did attempt to shield her. But in protecting her from the press, they damaged her credibility. Knowing what they know now, they might have done things differently. But this was a terrible day for the organization.

Jeannie Ghent acted as spokeswoman for the entertainer's family throughout the ordeal. "The surgery performed on her broken right leg was successful. The operation was considered necessary to clean broken glass from the area of Barbara's knee. Fortunately, there were no injuries to her face—not even a scratch," Ghent reported.

The Hendersonville police found that Mandrell and her children were wearing seat belts when the accident occurred. They credit the belts for saving three lives that night.

According to Police Lieutenant John Watson: "I'd certainly put my two cents on it. She and her two children were wearing theirs, but the other guy wasn't."

"She always insists they buckle up," Ghent claims.

"He was quiet but he had a lot of friends. He was serious-minded. He'd worked all day and come home to clean up," recalled Linda White, Mark's mother. "I don't think it was anything he was negligent about. I don't know if he had fallen asleep or what."

Louise jumped from the ambulance at the hospital. She was extremely protective. She reportedly shouted at the press, "Barbara has been there every time you've wanted her. So please turn the cameras off! She loves you. So please stop!"

Later, in a news conference after her sister had been transported to Baptist Hospital, Louise gave a general report. She said her sister was "more awake and alert now. She will be fine, and we ask for your prayers."

Jeannie Ghent gave more details. "Barbara spoke with Ken briefly this morning, and she also spoke with Louise. She is conscious and she is able to speak, but goes in and out of sleep."

So the news was not all bad for the Mandrells. There were serious injuries, but they would all make it. The news for Mark White's family was grim. "He was pronounced dead on arrival at Hendersonville Hospital,'' reported Hendersonville Police Chief David Key. ''The entire front end [of White's car] was ripped off the car,'' one witness said. ''You could tell there was a real impact. Her windshield was shattered and the hood was bashed in and pressed all the way up to the roof. It looked as though the driver must have really gotten hurt.''

''She wasn't even coherent when she arrived. She couldn't even recognize her own father,'' Ms. Pirtle, a spokesperson for Hendersonville Hospital, commented. She also reported that officials said the entertainer's injuries included a ''badly fractured thigh,'' which might take up to eight months to heal. ''It depends on how the doctors fix it,'' said Ms. Pirtle.

Asked about Barbara's state of mind, she explained that Ms. Mandrell ''was very confused and didn't know what had happened. She must have banged her head.''

So, the news was out. The deluge of interest and support from well-wishers had begun. Police Chief Key started to receive calls. ''Both country-music people and town folks were calling. The music business is a tightly knit community. Whenever one of them gets hurt, they're all concerned,'' he said.

''She's going to be all right,'' said Jeannie Ghent the next day.

By that time, the initial shock of the tragedy had worn off, and hard questions were being raised. Who was at fault? Was there driver negligence? Or was it just a chance occurrence, a freak accident? Lieutenant Watson was investigating. He reported, ''The biggest question was whether alcohol or drugs were involved, and they've both been ruled out,'' he said. ''There were no brakes applied.

''There's no indication at this time that either of them

was traveling over 40 miles an hour,'' Watson continued. "If they were going 50, it's going to be surprising."

"Jaime told me that Barbara had told them just a few seconds before the accident to put on their seat belts and they did,'' an eyewitness from Hendersonville told the press. She was one of the few eyewitnesses. She said she was a neighbor of Mandrell's.

Continuing what was to become the dominant theme of the post-wreck press coverage, the importance of seat belts, Jeannie Ghent said, "We feel this saved her life."

Once it was apparent that Barbara's injuries, however serious, were not life-threatening, many people, including the immediate family, were concerned whether or not the performer's injuries would affect her dancing or other aspects of her career.

When the issue was raised by the media, once again, Ghent responded. "We hope not. It will take time to tell. We'll have to wait and see how her leg heals. It was a clean break, thank goodness." Ever optimistic, even in crisis, the Mandrell organization was running true to form. Yet there were moments when everyone, including those closest to Barbara, still had grave concerns.

The AP printed an interview with Irby shortly after the wreck. He commented on reports of Barbara's loss of memory. This rumor, along with other more exaggerated reports, was beginning to circulate widely.

"I think the good Lord just kind of blocked out a section there,'' he said during a news conference. "She probably will never remember [the crash], according to what the doctors tell me. I would say her number one goal is to get well."

Dr. David S. Jones, an orthopedic surgeon at Baptist Hospital, performed the operation on her leg. He told reporters Barbara should shortly be on crutches or using a walker. He also felt she would eventually regain full use of her leg.

"The patient has a very strong will and very strong constitution and her spirit is one that lends itself to healing. She has done very well and has good support from her family," he said.

Jones went on to confirm that the leg injury, a break in the right femur, or thighbone, was a "fairly clean" simple fracture, which means the bone never protruded through the skin. Barbara also broke her right ankle and suffered some bruises, but there were no cuts on her face. Concluding on an upbeat note, Jones said, "We were able to realign the bone in its proper rotation and the exact length that it had been before."

Following surgery, the injured singer was moved from intensive care to a private room, where she was put under the care of an orthopedic nurse around-the-clock. With the public still clamoring for information, a special news conference was called by Dr. Jones three days following the crash.

The surgeon opened with a simple statement of the facts, delivered in the perfunctory post-operative press conference style so familiar to Americans: "She underwent major leg surgery at 7:00 P.M., Tuesday night. On the night of her original accident, September 11, she was taken to surgery and placed in traction with ropes and weights for the fracture of the right femur. The traction was to hold the bone at the proper length and to diminish pain. At this point, all traction apparatus has been removed. No complications have been encountered."

The main effort had been the placement of a metal rod in a four-inch incision above the singer's hip. Dr. Jones stated that it was "the size of a finger and a foot long."

The rod was implanted in the marrow of the bone across the fracture site to firmly secure the break.

"Fortunately, the fracture itself was a clean break in the midshaft of the bone. It did not come through the skin. It was not a compound fracture. The pieces fit together like a puzzle."

Dr. Jones then confirmed that they had been able to realign the bone in its proper location with the same length. In response to a question about the near-term outlook, he offered, "The plans are, medically, to have the patient out of bed in forty-eight hours, hopefully walking within three days." Later there would be "external support" (a walker) and lots of physical therapy. He also predicted a need for crutches for three or four months.

Barbara also suffered a head injury. Bizarre rumors about its nature and severity were flying. In an attempt to put an end to the speculation, Jones reported, "She has sustained a concussion, but she has been conscious and never in a coma. She was able to answer questions [following her admission to the hospital], but had severe headaches at times. She is coherent and seems to have a normal memory. Her face was not cut or scarred. Her minor bruises are already beginning to resolve.

"As far as I'm told, and medically speaking, all concerts and engagements should be canceled until the first of the year. I'm glad things are going as they are."

Jones credited the seat belt with saving Barbara's life "and preserving the ability to continue her career. It allowed her to slip forward enough to bang her right knee. That force transferred through and broke the thighbone. The lacerations to the knee have been cleaned and are doing well. I don't see any injury that she's had from which she will not recover."

He went on to explain that it would be at least eighteen

months before doctors would consider removing the metal rod. "It's not mandatory, but it can be done. If so, it could be done on a one-day admission."

During one of her lucid moments, when she was coherent enough to understand, Barbara was told about a huge get-well billboard erected by fans in Nashville. She also heard of others around the country, including one in Kansas, which was to have been her next tour date. The wreck, however, cost her that one. Fans seemed to understand. The billboards were their way of expressing something everyone wanted to say. Barbara saw them on TV and was very happy about it.

Meanwhile, a tremendous public outpouring of sympathy was creating logistical problems. Baptist had never seen anything like it before. The singer received over four hundred bouquets of flowers. "She was allowed one bouquet at a time while she was in intensive care," Irby said. "We saved all the cards for her and distributed the flowers throughout the hospital to other people's rooms. She's received four or five mailsacks full of mail."

The psychology of trauma is still largely unexplored territory. What happens when a person survives a terrible event like this is difficult to explain. We do know that survivors suffer guilt, fear, amnesia, lack of confidence, apathy. Barbara had all these symptoms and, if the truth were known, probably still does. No official word documents whether or not she receives psychological help as a result of her ordeal. One can only guess.

Barbara may never remember the exact sequence of events that led up to the point of impact. She can only reconstruct the accident from what she has been told. At her first public appearance following the crash, she gave an account of what eyewitnesses saw as she entered the emergency room. Although she spared the blood and gore, it still wasn't pretty.

"My father and my mother and my sister Louise were there when I got there. They've told me what I did. I was in excruciating pain. I was yelling at people, at the doctors. 'Get away from me!' I said. 'Leave me alone! Don't touch me!' I kept threatening them. 'I'll get my father in here!' They said I then doubled up my fist and *bam!* hit him good. Some time went by and then I hit the doctor again. Then I reached up my hand and put it on his cheek and was just 'loving him' and stroking his face. Then all of a sudden I went *bam* and hit him again!

"Many, many days later, after I was released, I called the doctor that I had hit to thank him so much for what he had done for me and to apologize to him. He assured me 'You had no idea that you were doing that, because of the concussion.'

"I don't have the words to tell you of the trauma, the emotional pains, the ups and downs. I am still not well, but I am getting better every day."

The outpouring of sentiment for the singer was overwhelming, unexpected and nearly unmanageable. The facilities at Baptist were soon overtaxed. Spokesperson Gil Caywood of the hospital staff described the problems and the procedures employed once the flowers arrived at the hospital: "What we're doing is we take them to the conference room where we're storing them, first off. Then we take them up to her suite, and we rotate them in and out every two to three hours. After Miss Mandrell gets a look at them, we take them out and bring the old ones to the pediatrics wing. Then we bring a batch of new ones up."

Caywood seemed to be overwhelmed by the sheer volume of the floral offerings. "Her room was absolutely covered with flowers. Some were just great big and others very small, tiny and dainty, every variety, every color, every shape.''

A Nashville reporter, Kay Jackson, managed to talk to an eyewitness soon after the collision, even before Barbara was released. The eyewitness recalled what happened: ''I was driving in the outside lane and she was in the center lane when she passed me. She was several car lengths ahead of me. I saw a puff of steam and realized there had been a collision. It was obvious that the driver of the other car was dead. There was no question in anybody's mind about that.''

When Miss Jackson asked about Barbara's condition at the scene, the eyewitness told her, ''When they took Barbara out of the car, she started moaning and that made me feel good because at least she was alive.''

The witness had somehow been able to speak to Jaime. This was remarkable due to the extent of Jaime's own injuries.

''Jaime told me that Barbara had told them just a few seconds before the accident to put on their seat belts and they did.'' The facts show now that it was a matter of several minutes instead of just seconds.

Louise became the dominant force in the family as the Mandrell clan attempted to get things under control. Things had always been well managed in the tight-knit family, but they had never been confronted with anything as serious as this before. Now Louise was taking charge, in many ways just as Barbara would have done. She stated in an interview following the accident, ''It'll be some time before Barbara gets back on the road because she does have a rather serious injury to her leg. It will take a little time, but she'll be fine.'' It was a shaky optimism that emerged. ''I appreciate, and I know Barbara would appreciate, everyone's prayers. And we also want to ask everyone, please while you're praying to pray for the White family.''

Irby told Mark Zabriskie of the *Banner*, ''She remembers the words to her songs.'' He also commented on Barbara's intense schedule and what she would be doing about it. ''We're helping concert producers get other performers booked to do her concerts, and Louise is taking several of the shows.''

The Mandrell organization had deliberately chosen not to keep things hush-hush during this time, but no great details were provided—only superficial information to keep the public at bay. This was so uncharacteristic that the fans were in shock. Barbara explained later at a news conference, ''The press was never lied to. But details about me were treated softly because I have senior citizens that are my fans that love me like I'm their own. And I have little bitty children that love me like I'm their best buddy. My husband, my father, my family were going through things that they did not want my fans to go through.''

It is generally agreed that it was Irby who decided to put a lid on things. The extent of the damage to Barbara's leg was underplayed. Being perennial troupers, the family rallied to the rescue. Country music's sweetheart was now in an extremely vulnerable position. They would guard her until she could face the public on her own.

In the case of a public figure like Mandrell, privacy is something of a luxury. It is difficult to achieve, even in ordinary times. In this case, it was out of the question. The family had drawn the line, but the press and fans were trying to cross it.

This course of action caused the star considerable damage. The entire career of Barbara Mandrell had been built around intimacy. Closeness to her fans was a virtue Barbara celebrated. Proximity to their favorite star was something her fans cherished. This special relationship was achieved through Barbara's special gift for personal contact. Now, at the height of her trauma, there had been an interruption of the flow of news. The irony was that this was a time when her fans needed the most information about her. Whether Irby's decision was right or wrong, it has to be understood that the pressure of the circumstances must have been enormous.

This was a tragedy in many senses. The fact that there was a fatality was a blot on the name she had worked so hard to keep clean. A life had been taken. In some people's minds, there would always be questions of guilt, or blame. It was ruled that Barbara was not at fault in the death of Mark White. Yet a cloud now hung over her. Could she get past it? These and many other fundamental questions were going through the minds of those at the top of the Mandrell organization.

Another incalculable element of the tragedy was the loss to Barbara of something deep within her, the gift for human expression. The accident took away her edge. Her confidence was more than shaken; a deep fissure had scarred it. She had lost the dynamic intensity that had pushed her so far so fast.

Basically, Barbara was an intense workaholic. The accident cut into her ability to go, to do. She had been the last word in self-sufficiency. Do or die. Now she was helpless. To a temperament such as hers, this vulnerable condition can be fatal.

It led her to second-guess her motives. Surely it exercised a tremendous braking influence on the motives of everyone connected to her life and career. She was an industry, generating millions of dollars, employing dozens of people. In the most crass of considerations, she was a mainstay of consumerism. But the whole machine had ground to a halt as Barbara lay disabled.

The weeks of suffering were coupled with despair, depression, fits of anger. Coping with the lengthy process of healing, she drifted aimlessly. Soul-searching was of little help; introspection only compounded her problem. Convalescence is an exhausting and devastating process for someone like Barbara, so used to perpetual motion. In most cases, however, it is the body's way of making repairs and going on. But regeneration takes time, and Barbara wasn't used to that.

Upon learning of the fate of the other driver, she underwent a process of grieving. The young man had died. Being a warm and caring person, she attached a lot of emotional baggage to the fact. Grief has several definite stages: The initial shock soon gives way to denial. Anger and depression take control, and it requires great determination to overcome their debilitating effects. Eventual acceptance is by no means certain.

It is easy to picture the fragile blonde singer in her plight, lying in a hospital bed, frustrated by forced immobility. She was bewildered, besieged by feelings that changed with every moment. Imagining herself in the other driver's place was unavoidable. Fortunately she could not remember the accident itself. Barbara was lucid only fitfully, lapsing in and out of consciousness. Her emotions were unstable. Her capacity for thinking and decision-making was jarred. She could barely recognize her family.

The long-term effects of the trauma were no less devastating. They thwarted her drive. Her enthusiasm was gone. Her very existence was threatened.

Barbara made a living based on her raw drive and energy. These were the natural resources she used to get where she was. Now they seemed to have vanished. They had propelled her to the top. She'd won countless awards and achieved remarkable commercial success. Her popularity seemed boundless. She could probably have run for elected office and won. But all her vitality was stymied in the wake of the accident.

She was down. She was in a tough spot, a place she had never been before. But in fact Barbara had so many things going for her in spite of the long odds. Her energy was really only dormant. The physical prowess was still there, only waiting for release. It is important to remember that she had been in great physical shape before the accident. She was more than a stand-up entertainer, she was a dancer with great stamina. And those who knew her best knew she was also a fighter, one who wouldn't accept being anything but a winner. The disciplined habits cultivated in the course of a long, successful career were to prove to be powerful medicine.

Deep within her lived a spirit that knew no limits. Waiting for a moment of challenge, it slowly awakened. The same verve that brought her through so many other challenges was now being channeled into her recovery. Redirected by necessity, it would bring about the comeback of one of the most popular entertainers of the early 1980s.

This flghting spirit was already beginning to rally her toward recovery. She wasn't even aware of it, yet she was planning a comeback. She might not be able to put the pieces back together again exactly as they were, but she *would* get back.

6

Recovery

"I THANK GOD I'm alive!" was Barbara's triumphant procla-
mation at her first public appearance after the accident.
She had been in the hospital for nineteen days. She had
been silent for several months after her release. She had
gone through several operations. Now she was back.

Everything in her life had been at a standstill. Her entire
career was on hold. Her recovery was paramount, while
everything else moved into the background. But it was
frustrating to sit back and read the media accounts of her
progress. She had been off the road, attempting to analyze
the complex situation created by the accident.

It was now January 1985. A whole new phase of her
career was unfolding. She had never been subjected to so
much criticism. She had always been able to see the
positive side of things. Her carefully crafted image, and
her cool, controlled public persona had made her the public's darling, the sweetheart of the media rodeo. But that
was before the accident. Now she was taking her lumps.

The recovery process involved much more than physical healing. While drawing on her inner reserves, Barbara was constantly planning, one might even say plotting, to get back. In a way the accident served as a catalyst for her to go through the process of redefining herself, clarifying her sense of who she was and why she was alive. It probably would have happened anyway, but the trauma speeded up the process. She was ready to emerge like a butterfly from the cocoon. She had been recovering physically. Contemplating her psychological health, however, had been more problematic. She realized that her reemergence would be painful. The result of all this analysis was her decision that she would be able to face it only if she took the initiative.

And now Barbara was white-hot, prepared for anything they could throw at her. She had been preparing for January 3, 1985, as much as for any concert. Possible responses to anticipated questions were thoroughly explored. She was ready. She knew her lines. Barbara would meet the press head-on. At the Opryland Hotel, where the conference was to be held, she hobbled in on crutches. Someone who didn't know what lay behind those blue eyes might have felt pity. The petite singer slowly made her way to the microphone. She was at home now, more so than in the stillness of a convalescent room, far more than when sitting quietly alone, thinking of what she might say.

She had called the conference as a way to respond to the deluge of requests for interviews received during the past three months. Rather than play favorites, she would speak to them as a group.

"I'm so happy to see you all," she began. Tears welled in her eyes, and in those of the audience. Master of the game, she disarmed any would-be critic who might have lurked in the crowd. "Today is my first public appearance since the accident, and I've been on an emotional high all day. Forgive me if I skip around too much or am not very articulate. I am certainly trying to do my best. I've cried a lot. I'm still pretty emotional.''

She had them right where she wanted them.

Her memory had returned slowly sometime after September 25, she said. She had been released from the hospital five days later. She was still involved in ongoing physical therapy.

Questions about her health and career status persisted. Could she regain her abilities? Or were the injuries too extensive to overcome? After no direct word about her condition for months, the time had finally come to speak out.

''One of the reasons for this press conference is because my office has been getting so many requests for interviews with me regarding my accident and my career. And because I've been treated so wonderfully in the twenty-five years I've been in show business by the people of the press—and I didn't have the strength to do individual interviews with everyone—I decided on the press conference, hoping that it would please all of you . . . and that it would allow the public to see that I'm back among the living.

''There have been many, many rumors since the accident—that I had lost a leg, that I had a disfigured face. Or the extreme opposite—that I'm well and why am I not back at work? There have also been rumors that I'm quitting show business.'' With a self-satisfied chuckle, she said, ''They don't know me very well.'' The old sense of humor seemed still to be there, although it was now flavored with a more somber tone.

She had been given ample opportunity to think about her next statements. They were delivered with evangelistic zeal. ''I say this not as Barbara Mandrell, but as a friend.

Please tell the people of this country," she appealed directly to the folks in the room, "from the bottom of my heart because I love them—'Wear your seat belts!' I was not a seat belt user . . . I was a fool . . . I thought it was absurd. I'm living today to tell you it does make a difference . . . and with all my heart, I'm hoping and praying that people start using their seat belts!''

Her tone was obviously one appropriate to the keeping of promises made in another setting, in different circumstances. She was now making good on a pledge. She would tell the seat belt story as an ardent advocate. She would get results.

She related the moments before the crash and the last things she remembered—three kids perched on the back of an open tailgate. She had told her children, "Let's fasten our seat belts; then we'll be safe." Fifteen minutes later she proved to be correct. It was a tough way to go to become a believer. "It is the opinion of the doctors that we probably, all three of us, would have been killed had we not had those seat belts. It was God's will that we had our seat belts on."

She unveiled her plans publicly to promote the wearing of seat belts, including some video spots for the National Traffic Safety Council. Her convictions were firmly cemented, with good reason. She continued, "I'm very grateful that I can do that . . . I thank God I'm alive. I don't have words to tell you of the trauma, the physical pain and the tremendous emotional ups and downs I've been through. A concussion affects the emotions; it's a medical fact."

Despite the obvious emotion, Barbara's manner was controlled, her delivery impeccably professional. It would have been difficult not to have been impressed by her courage and determination. She seemed more fragile than one would have expected, and that only increased the admiration of her audience. "It has been a difficult ordeal. I have had to fight. I'm not well yet; but I'm getting well. There have been times when not being able to be energetic and active has brought me to tears. Then there were times when it didn't bother me at all. But if you're not well and not feeling good, then you don't want to do anything. I watched a lot of TV, read, visited and planned."

Barbara was verbalizing what everyone sensed she had been going through. It was in a way satisfying to hear her say it.

She commented on her collection of over four hundred floral arrangements—a Baptist Hospital record. "And now I have a humdinger of a basket collection!" Shades of the old Mandrell.

She continued, "I think a lot of people know how much I love my fans. But I don't think I knew how much they love me back."

One of her fans was the President of the United States. He called from Air Force One to wish her well. Former President Jimmy Carter and a host of other government people also had telephoned. In humble fashion, true to her former self, she replied, "I know those men are busy men. I'm a real patriot. So I felt like a big shot."

Could she get back in the saddle soon? Could she perform, dance, sing? The question arose in the taping of a Barbara Walters special. In response she stated, "That'll be easy. I won't have to dance." This answer engendered doubts about her physical ability. She was quick to pick up on the murmurs. When could she resume? "I wish I knew the answer to that. Dr. Jones says I am ahead of schedule. But it's as if you were building a new house. You can't exactly say the date the house will be finished. I have healing to do. I have decided not to put any pressure on myself. I'm a go-getter enough to know . . . I'll know when I'm ready. But when I do my next television special and when I do Las Vegas, yes, I will dance! I definitely will. And it won't be too terribly long.'' Barbara's tone was positive, her voice strong. But the words, although forthright, sounded just a bit uncertain, as if she were trying to convince the reporters and maybe even herself. A little bravado goes a long way.

At this point she launched into a promo spot for her next TV special, set to air a few days later. The poor timing almost ruined the effect she'd just created. It provoked more than a little suspicion. Was this really hype for a show? If she was thrown off balance by the reaction, she gave no sign of it: "I want you to watch, no kidding! This one is not just saying it's special; it is a special. This is a super show . . . I'm so proud of it. This is me back to being Barbara Mandrell, and just pushing.'' If it was a confession, it certainly was not a revelation. No one was surprised.

The dominant theme of the media questioning quickly emerged. How had she changed? She responded, "I've always been a person to say we're really not here on the face of this earth that long. But I think I kinda meant it as a figure of speech. Now I know for a fact that it's just a twinkling of an eye; that's all we are here for.

"My seriousness about my family, my fans, the people I love . . . After the accident I thought of so many people I love and thought, why haven't I just looked them in the eye and said *I love you?* I was always happy to be alive, but I never realized what a blessing it is and how grateful we should be. Because we're never promised tomorrow, just today.

"And most of all—and you mamas and daddies know this—more than anything I'm so thankful that my family and my children are there . . . And I have prayed often for the family of the boy who died."

Ken stood behind her as she delivered the address. He appeared dark, severe. He held her coat almost protectively, looking very much out of place.

The next month another announcement concerning Barbara Mandrell made its way to the nation's newspapers. The diminutive country singer was expecting a child. Now thirty-six, the entertainer stated, "We're shocked and thrilled to death. We've been through such serious hard times that it's nice to have some good news. We're overjoyed."

In informing her parents, Barbara decided to tease them a bit. She called and asked, "I understand you're going to be grandparents again." Mary replied, "Well, not that I know of."

"You mean Irlene isn't pregnant?"

"No, I don't think so."

"Well, is Louise expecting?" her daughter continued.

"No, she hasn't told us."

Barbara could stand it no longer. "Well, then, it must be me." She laughed. Finally, Mary caught on.

"We thank God for it. We've put it in God's hands and said, 'Thank you.' I'm just stunned and so happy. I didn't expect something wonderful like this."

Since her news conference, she had been trying her best to put the wheels back on things once more. Barbara had become a disciple of seat belt use; she had crusaded non-stop. "My main thing in life right now is working toward encouraging people to use seat belts. Prior to the wreck, I resented seat belts for stupid reasons, like they mess up your clothes. God just wanted us to live, I guess."

She became relentless on the subject. In April, she turned lobbyist to the state legislature. Trading on her stature as a celebrity, she used it to gain a voice with the politicians. She made a personal appearance, urging Tennessee lawmakers to adopt a mandatory law requiring seat belt use. She was being supported by many in the effort, including then Governor Lamar Alexander.

She was asked to testify before a joint House-Senate subcommittee studying the problem. She had been asked by at least six other state legislatures to testify. Her home state was the first stop.

She began, "I was not a seat belt user, period. If we weren't wearing seat belts—and all experts have told us this—all three of us would have been killed. I'm living to tell you that it makes a difference."

Although the more cynically inclined might have felt Barbara was merely posturing, trying to cash in on her accident, those closest to her had a different opinion. Irby commented that she feels "strongly enough that when they were in Tahoe and a limousine pulled up without seat belts, she wouldn't ride in it. They had to call another one."

In 1977, Tennessee had been the first state to pass legislation making the use of child restraint devices mandatory. But Barbara was convinced the legislation was not the final solution to the problem. She stated, "That's only half the job. Why should we make them orphans, if we don't put them [seat belts] on the parents?"

She went into further detail, hoping to drive the point home: "The impact of my crash was estimated to be in excess of 100 miles per hour by the police. . . . It's not true that it only affects yourself, the one person. Maybe there are the children, maybe there is a mother and a father, maybe you have a brother or a sister. There's somebody there that loves you and it affects them."

She concluded her plea to the legislature, "You have the power to pass laws for good in spite of what the public thinks. You have the numbers and statistics. Because of your caring and expertise, you can save our lives. I'm really not trying to butter you up. I'm telling you the truth."

The current Governor of Tennessee, Ned McWherter, then Speaker of the House in the state legislature, finally came around. He had previously been opposed to the bill. Barbara said, "I think that was the biggest, most loving thing you could do—to say you were wrong."

Graciously accepting Barbara's praise, McWherter said simply, "I was wrong. That's what it's all about—education and training. I was wrong."

Mandrell responded, "So was I. I was not a seat belt user. I'm still healing. I've been told of people who are wearing their seat belts because of our experience. The pain is worth it."

Tennessee subsequently became one of several states to pass mandatory seat belt laws. Barbara can take much of the credit for giving the campaign for legislation the impetus needed to swing the vote around.

Continuing to hammer away at the public conscience, she made a dramatic trip to see her ruined Jaguar, which had been stored near her house. It was emotionally very difficult but necessary. Fragments of suppressed memory welled up in her. Disjointed thoughts and painful images seemed to flood her consciousness.

She looked at the wreckage in awe. The Jaguar is a study in the physics of high-speed impact. The front of the car was gone. There is a concave space where the driver's side had been. The steering wheel is crumpled. Shattered windshield glass is strewn around the dash area. Barbara found it difficult to explain her feelings. "I looked inside and I can't describe it. It's a miracle I still have my legs.

My voice is still hot, powerful, big. When I get behind the mike, the voice is strong.''

Barbara's desire to return to performing was even stronger now. She began making plans for a comeback tour even before she left the hospital. By February, it had begun to come together. She also battled a new fear, one she never had before. "I'm nervous about facing the stage again. I never thought I would be, but I am."

The months passed into the summer of 1985. On the eve of the first anniversary of the collision, and near the end of her pregnancy, the news was out. Barbara Mandrell was suing the family of the accident victim for $10.3 million.

While the press still buzzed over that news, the country singer was admitted to Baptist Hospital after suffering labor pains. The family spokesperson, Jeannie Ghent, took charge again: "She's had some minor labor pains. They're planning on doing a cesarean tomorrow morning if she doesn't have the baby overnight. Hopefully everything will go as scheduled."

Hospital spokesman Bob Johnson added: "She has been admitted. It's no emergency. She's ready to deliver. She's real close."

Progress reports were issued in a steady stream. The Mandrell machine had learned a painful lesson after the crash by distancing itself from the press; that mistake would not be repeated. Jeannie Ghent made it perfectly clear: "That's the agreement of the family, that they will release the condition report."

In answer to a reporter's question, Ghent commented on the condition of the expectant father. "Ken is Mr. Stability. He's anxious. He only wants a healthy baby. They have a boy and a girl and I just hope Barbara doesn't have any more problems than she's been having."

Dr. Newt Lovvorn was delivering. Jeannie advised the persistent press, "I think he'll make a statement in the morning."

Remembering the deluge of calls from the previous year, Baptist spokesperson Johnson stated, "I've gotten a few calls already. The family will make all announcements, not Baptist." That was a wise choice. The hospital, too, would not repeat its own mistakes.

On September 6, 1985, Nathaniel Mandrell Dudney was born, weighing seven pounds and seven ounces. The Mandrell organization had a statement ready. "They're all so excited. They said Barbara was doing fine and everything was OK."

On the same day, the story of the lawsuit finally exploded. The Mandrell case was presented aptly through her lawyer, Aubrey Harwell: "Barbara was badly injured and is still suffering as a result of those injuries received in the car crash.

"Medical expenses have been significant, but the largest losses have been from public-performance contracts she was unable to fulfill. I would estimate some $6 million to $8 million."

Ken Dudney, usually quiet, stepped in. "The suit basically involves matters pertaining to insurance."

The years of public trust Barbara had so carefully built dissolved in less than a week. The press conference, the crusades for seat belts, the charity engagements were all nullified by the press, who seemed to jump on the story of a wealthy superstar suing the poor family of a dead accident victim. Sympathy and flowers had turned to contempt almost overnight.

A fickle public leaped to denounce Barbara's greed. Letters poured in to the editors of papers all over the state. Local talk shows were inundated with irate calls. For the first time in her career, genuine hostility was directed at the baffled singer. While the issue raged, she remained dumbfounded.

Harwell commented on the vehemence of public reaction. "We've taken an unusual amount of heat on this. And Barbara has really been hurt. I hate to see anyone blasted like this."

Barbara had just delivered her third child. She had undergone a cesarean section and was still on the mend. Nathaniel came into the world in a storm of controversy.

"Here she is, just after a cesarean section," the attorney continued, "and this sort of heat takes place." He seemed outraged.

The suit accused the deceased teen of "negligence." The singer was asking for $10 million in damages. Matthew was to receive $200,000 for injuries, while Jaime was to get $100,000. Ken was seeking $25,000 for the "loss of the services, companionship, consortium and society of his wife."

Attempting to defuse the outcry, Harwell explained the singer's intentions further. "Our position is, we want the insurance companies that Barbara and Ken pay tens of thousands of dollars in insurance premiums every year to to meet their obligations. Procedurally, in the state of Tennessee, it's the only way you can collect."

The Nashville attorney stated that public sentiment had been running against him. "People have called me up and cussed me out, called me all kinds of no-good-so-and-so's."

Suddenly, in a process no one in Barbara's camp seemed to understand, the roles had been reversed. Mark White had become the hero, Mandrell the villain.

Banner writer Jim Henry's contention was that the Whites were "scared to death." His September 19th story contradicted previous reports that the Whites were understanding of the dilemma. "The Whites' necks are stuck out." C. L. Rogers, a Gallatin attorney, responded: "They said they've heard this or that about the suit, and that it isn't aimed at them but they don't know anything for sure. They told me, 'All we know is we've been sued for $10 million.'"

Richard White, father of the victim, was named in the suit. Technically White could be held liable for the charges. But Mandrell's people reiterated that the suit was aimed at the insurance companies.

The firm that carried her insurance agreed with the singer. Her insurance man, Robert Frost, stated: "I think they've gotten a bad rap. I'm the guy that's going to be giving them the check, not the Whites."

Meanwhile, attorney Rogers responded. "We hope—and I believe—that Barbara Mandrell is not interested in any assets from the Whites. We have their statement to that effect, but that's all we've got."

Would the entertainer sue the family and take them down? Was she getting bad advice? Had injuries impaired her judgment? Some thought so.

A local headline called the new sport in Nashville "Barbara-Bashing." One caller to a local talk show articulated a common theme: "But if she gets a judgment against the daddy, he'll be bankrupt. There she is with all that money, trying to get what little the family has."

The public perception of her now was highly charged, and clearly negative. It bordered on animosity. Rich entertainer takes money of dead boy's family. It wasn't exactly accurate, but that's the way it was being viewed. The public-relations damage would be hard to undo.

Hendersonville was Barbara's hometown. In spite of its proximity to a large metropolitan area, it was still Small Town USA. There was a gossipy flavor to the stories that were circulating. The local people were used to living with celebrities nearby. This was a heyday for them.

While a friend to her fans around the world, the Barbara Mandrell of Hendersonville is somewhat elusive. The neighbors rarely see her. Not many store owners recall her visits. A few confirmed that she would often pull in at an all-night gas station on the way out before a date. This was usually in the middle of the night.

The locals really did not have personal contact with her. No wonder they took issue with her. Things had been bad. Now they seemed worse. The image was going . . . going . . . gone.

In times past, when she had been down and out, Barbara had gone on the road for strength. That could be the answer. A tour, with its adoring fans and the exhilaration of performance, might get her mind off the hostility and help restore her equilibrium. After all, it had been many months since she had done anything remotely resembling a concert.

So much had happened in the preceding year. The birth of Nathaniel, the accident, and the lawsuit seemed inextricably tied together in Barbara's memory. It was a difficult period for her. She lost interest in almost everything, even in things that had always appealed to her. Normally, her appetite for work is insatiable, her drive to succeed overwhelming. She loved her work and thought she couldn't live without it. But after the accident, she seemed like another person. Even her love of reading—everything from the Bible to autobiographies and Louis L'Amour westerns—suffered. Suddenly, she didn't even want to listen to the radio.

The anniversary of the accident was traumatic. She tried to lose herself in the baby, but kept thinking about the young man who hit her car, and the pain his parents must feel. Like most of us who've never lost a child, she couldn't conceive what such pain must be like. She found herself wondering how they managed to cope with the tragedy. Her heart goes out to them and she prays for them.

Even after a year, Barbara's memory of the hospital stay was still hazy. Combined with a concussion, injections of Demerol and morphine had dulled her senses and blocked out her awareness of events and surroundings. There were few recollections because she had virtually no conscious experience of the hospital confinement.

In an interview some time ago, she said, "I wasn't aware of anything. I guess in this way I was blessed. All I know of that period is what my family tells me. My husband says I talked a lot, screaming, yelling and crying. And I was very demanding . . . I'd look at the clock on the wall of Intensive Care at Baptist Hospital and say, 'Okay, I have to get ready now—it's show time!' I was obsessed with the idea I was on the road."

She eventually was taken off the painkillers. Beginning publicly to come to grips with that aspect of her hospitalization, she demonstrated that it is a painful experience to recall. She told one reporter, "I don't have the words to describe what it was like. I'd always been gutsy about pain, but not that kind of pain . . . All my doctors were very anti-drugs, and I thank the Lord that they knew how anti-drugs I am. Otherwise I'd probably have become addicted."

When her pain persisted longer than expected, her doctors eventually prescribed Darvocet. Because it was safer than other painkillers, she was able to use it until she was five months pregnant. She was also subject to dramatic mood swings, sometimes screaming at her children without provocation. Later, she realized that if Ken had ever treated her the way she treated him during that period, she might have left him. But at the time, she felt no guilt.

Her ankle is still damaged, and she still doesn't know if full mobility will ever return. She will admit that she's not as strong as she used to be, and this is not easy for a woman who used to arm-wrestle men and even win on occasion.

She and Ken don't talk about the accident very much. According to Barbara, Ken doesn't want to remember it. She had taken so much of the pain and anger out on him, because it is always easiest to ventilate such feelings with those you love. Barbara is used to her independence, and still treasures it, but the accident has given her a fuller appreciation of her family, and especially of Ken.

Severe stress does take its toll on relationships. It's tempting, but pointless and probably unfair, to speculate about the two of them and the months following the trauma. Such times require patience, healing and love. Was it real? Had they made it? Or were they still not out of the woods? And, perhaps most to the point, was it anyone's business?

Barbara's level of candor seems to have increased in the aftermath of the accident and the storm of outrage that greeted news of the lawsuit. She is now more willing, and apparently better able, to risk a moment of intimacy with her fans. In discussing some of the most personal aspects of the accident and her period of recovery, she has been strikingly open. In this, there is a hint that she is truly different from a pre-accident Barbara Mandrell.

She had to break up her band during her recovery period since there were no concert dates for them. It was a difficult decision for her. She didn't let the band go for several months, even though she knew she wouldn't be back on stage for quite a while. Some of the band had been with her for ten years.

On the most problematic question, her return to her craft, Barbara seemed to be regaining her confidence. At a press conference, she announced, "I'm only satisfied when that sweat starts dripping and I'm really pushing it. Then I feel, 'Yes, I'm giving the person who bought the ticket a show I'm proud of.' I'll wear tall boots to give support around my ankles and then I'll work like normal; but I won't be dancing like I did on my CBS and HBO specials."

She went on to say, "I still hope I love it. I'm a little nervous about the tour, but that will probably disappear once we get started. The moment I drive out of those gates out there, I belong to the people. I've given shows when I felt so bad I could lay down and die. I've performed with a one-hundred-and-six-degree fever from viral pneumonia. But the public never saw anything but a smile. I would never set foot on stage unless I could give one hundred percent to my audience."

One of Barbara's earliest publicity shots, taken in the late sixties.
Courtesy of The Country Music Foundation

Barbara Mandrell on stage at country music's Mecca, The Grand Ole Opry, in the mid-seventies. *Courtesy of The Country Music Foundation*

Barbara makes a point of attending the annual Country Music Fair, and spends hours signing autographs and mingling with her fans. *Courtesy of The Country Music Foundation*

By 1983 there was no doubt that Barbara Mandrell had established herself as one of the biggest names in the country music business. Here she is with two equally well-known contemporaries, Ronnie Milsap and Larry Gatlin. *Courtesy of the John St. John collection*

Barbara in her dressing-room trailer during a break in the filming of her TV show, "Barbara Mandrell and the Mandrell Sisters." *Courtesy of Nancy Barr/Retna, Ltd.*

Irby and Mary Mandrell often visited their daughters on the set of "Barbara Mandrell and the Mandrell Sisters." They're shown here with Irlene, Barbara, and Louise. *Courtesy of The Country Music Foundation*

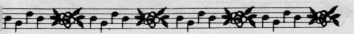

Barbara and George Jones accepting awards from The Academy of Country Music. *Courtesy of Rex Features Ltd.*

Barbara accepts the "Worst Dressed Woman Award" from the notorious fashion critic Mr. Blackwell in 1984. *Courtesy of Nancy Barr/Retna, Ltd.*

Barbara Mandrell performing at Fan Fair in the early eighties. *Courtesy of The Country Music Foundation*

Barbara and Ken arrive at an awards banquet in Los Angeles in the mid-eighties. The gentleman on the left is unidentified. *Courtesy of The Country Music Foundation*

June 10, 1985. Barbara Mandrell, in the sixth month of her third pregnancy, and nine months after the accident that almost took her life, returns to the concert stage in an emotional performance. *Courtesy of the John St. John collection*

The birth of Nathaniel Mandrell Dudney on September 6, 1985, signaled the beginning of a new period of happiness for Barbara and her family. This portrait was taken shortly after Nathaniel's birth and shows Barbara surrounded by her husband, Ken, as well as Matthew and Jaime. *Courtesy of Mandrell Country*

Throughout the seventies and eighties, Barbara Mandrell made hundreds of television appearances. This shot is from one of her most recent. *Courtesy of the John St. John collection*

Having fun in Aspen. Barbara and former White House kid Steven Ford. *Courtesy of Nancy Barr/Retna, Ltd.*

Fame makes strange and
varied bedfellows. Here is
Barbara with actress
Patricia Neal and former
White House press
secretary James Brady.
*Courtesy of Barry
Talesnick/Retna, Ltd.*

Roy Rogers, Dale Evans,
Barbara Mandrell, and one
huge birthday cake!
*Courtesy of Ralph
Dominguez, Globe Photos*

Four of Country Music's Queens gather together for a special song-
fest: Barbara, Minnie Pearl, Tammy Wynette, and Loretta Lynn.
Courtesy of Globe Photos

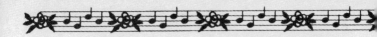

Barbara Mandrell today. *Courtesy of Mandrell Country*

7

Family

"I'M A VERY selfish person when it comes to my family," Barbara Mandrell once said. "I owe it not just to them but to myself to be with them."

She knows that her career has, in many ways, been hardest on Ken, about whom she said, "I have to respect him to love him. Although we don't have any hang-ups about sex roles—we think of ourselves as equals in just about every way—he's very much the husband. I know he's more intelligent than I am."

When they were still newlyweds she had been away from him on tour. Reflecting on the separation, she commented, "Those four months were some of the most difficult and lonely days in my life." It was so bad, she soon agreed to give up life on the road and become a housewife. Now she had to adjust to being a homebody. "I loved it! During that whole period when we were together every day I never once missed performing, being on stage."

The military short-circuited those happy times. Ken was

called up on active duty. After this came Barbara's famous sojourn at the Opry and her plea to her dad to manage her.

For his part, Ken has been considerate of his wife's career. Barbara understands the sacrifices he has made for her sake, and acknowledges his moral support. He has to share a part of her with thousands of others night after night. He has, however, confided that he has been troubled by feelings of inadequacy. "But Barbara was wise and helped me over troubled times."

"I'm a very independent person and so is Ken," Barbara has said. "We're both opinionated and our opinions are strong. Sure, we'll get into an argument and yell and scream at each other. That way we get it out, and everything blows over. Besides, there's no depth to a marriage without fights and rough spots. If you want your marriage and family to survive, you have to work at it."

When do they have time for that work? Her schedule is a hectic whirl, far from what most would consider a normal family life. The pattern is characterized by frequent long trips away. Public appearances take up a considerable amount of her time, and concerts take still more. Ken has his business trips and other obligations of his own. In a way, they live in two separate worlds. The odds make it seem difficult for them to keep it together.

For Barbara, the frequent separations are the most difficult aspect of her career. Most performers agree that it never gets any easier. Despite the old saw, Barbara does not believe that absence makes the heart grow fonder. And privacy is virtually nonexistent. Insanely comic rumors often fly in the tabloids. Tales of Elvis's ghost and Liz's next husband are staples, of course, but even Barbara Mandrell has to contend with gossip.

A few years ago, the gossip columns carried a story about Barbara dating Dodgers catcher Steve Yeager. At first, she found it amusing. Steve and his wife, Gloria, are good friends of both Ken and Barbara. The story received wide coverage. On one occasion, all four of them went out to dinner in Los Angeles. The next day one newspaper carried a headline that read "Barbara Mandrell seen with Steve Yeager"—as if neither of their spouses was present.

Awhile later, Barbara went down to the Dodgers' spring training camp in Florida. She loves playing softball but isn't much of a hitter, so Yeager offered to coach her to improve her performance at the plate. She worked hard, and after some practice, she was hitting fast balls at 70–80 miles per hour.

After a practice session one afternoon, a reporter from the *National Enquirer* came up to Yeager and asked him if it were true that he was seeing Mandrell. Steve and Barbara found it funny for a while, but when the rumor persisted it started to irritate both of them. Such intrusions are one of the hazards of celebrity and there isn't much one can do about it, but there are many times when the line between personal and public life is ignored by the tabloids.

Mandrell insists she is just an old-fashioned country girl, a one-man woman. The bottom line for both her and Ken is that they are married for life. They made that decision very early and are determined to stick to it, no matter what demands her career might impose, and despite the inge-nuity of rumormongers.

As if their careers didn't make demands enough on their energies and attention, they also have three children who have their own needs. Children take a great deal of time, time for the usual social activities that are so large a part of a normal kid's upbringing, and time for them to be taught about life. They need advice, support, role models.

Barbara once talked about the difficulty of arranging

their time. She said, ''We steal our moments. If I'm at the recording studio, I'll have the kids come over for lunch, and we'll sneak in a few video games.'' She knows the kids have had unusual lives, but she believes they have survived unscathed. ''These kids were practically raised on a tour bus. They love it.''

It must be a pretty exciting lifestyle at times. Jaime was featured on her mom's TV show in several skits. ''She didn't want to do it at first, and I didn't want to push her. But she'd read the lines with me at home and she was amazingly good. But I'd ask her to audition and she'd say, 'No ma'am.' Finally, I realized I hadn't told her she would get paid, so I said, 'Jaime, you know you get lots of money to do this?' Then she auditioned.''

How does Barbara Mandrell handle everyday motherhood? There are no magic formulas. She tries the same things every other mother tries. She's honest with her kids. She doesn't know much about drugs and the kids realize that. She is sheltered and hopes they're sheltered too. No one would be more shocked than Barbara if the kids got involved with drugs; most parents feel the same way about their kids.

Barbara and Ken both come from stock that sticks together, thick or thin. Even though they have experienced enormous financial and career success, they seem unspoiled. Decency, respect and decorum are just words to a lot of celebrities, but the Mandrells are not ordinary celebrities. They epitomize those traditional values so often lacking among entertainers.

They are a clan. Each member of that clan has woven his or her own identity, using individual threads to contribute to the larger pattern. The third generation is now making its mark. In the public limelight, the kids are bound to take a shot at musical careers sooner or later.

But all of it, music and Mandrell mystique, stems from the original Mandrells, Irby and Mary. Their desire to showcase their music, with that of their daughters, launched it all. Today, the Mandrell family name stands as a monument to Irby and Mary in many ways.

Nathaniel has yet to taste the flavor of success through public recognition, but he is currently enjoying its benefits in tangible ways as a result of his family name. The circumstances of his birth, and the subsequent publicity, have already thrust him into the public eye.

The Mandrells of the 1980s have come a long way from the Mandrells of a few decades ago. More than just a family, they are a corporate entity, bidding fair to become an empire. The family business has become the family *as* business—a conglomerate of media interests, talent and personalities. Its stock-in-trade is the shrewd manipulation of its public image. In an electronic age, they have had phenomenal popularity and spectacular recognition.

On close examination, however, it is difficult to grasp what makes the fabric of this tapestry so colorful, so bright. What is the secret of their success? As with an Impressionist painting, the closer one gets, the harder it is to see. The details blur, the edges disappear on minute scrutiny; the actual paint and brushstrokes on the canvas of the masterpiece seems rather ordinary.

Dad, an ordinary Houston policeman, turns ordinariness into a musical act that takes the nation by storm virtually from the beginning. The little country girl with the blonde hair and a big smile now directs a multi-million-dollar-a-year enterprise. Mom, the sisters, the kids, the extended family—all are part of the picture too.

From that very first request, that Irby manage her career, Barbara has never faltered in boosting her family. She kept her dad on even after the big-time account men and high-powered agencies took over. Ken still plays a major role in the business. Her kids are included in as many ways as she can contrive for them to be.

During the early days of poverty, they managed to put a high priority on togetherness. Kinship and camaraderie became the principal virtues of an appealing lifestyle. In the midst of strange, new environments, they had an uncommon bond: a celebration of what being a Mandrell was all about. They never lost it.

Even now, they find time to spend holidays together. When work dictates they be apart, they at least work on the same types of projects. They perform benefits and celebrity charity events together.

And even if they are not physically together, they stay bound by the code that the family comes first: The Mandrell family is a dinosaur in the computer age, an era cursed with a fifty-percent divorce rate. Irby and Mary have been together for many years. The children follow suit: the Dudneys; R. C. Bannon and Louise. Marriage is foremost among the set of traditional values they hold in common. Another is their protectiveness of each other. The old adage "blood is thicker than water" applies here. They are kin, and everyone else is an outsider.

Louise is the second oldest of Irby and Mary's children. As with the middle child in most families, she is not as aggressive as her older sister. She is less outgoing, but no less talented. According to one report, she had to beg Barbara to give her a shot on the show. This seems hard to believe, knowing how clannish they seem to be. Nevertheless, she did make the jump—a quantum leap from mere pretty face in the back-up band to headliner in her own right. She now commands her own array of fans. She has launched her career, which has really very little to do with Barbara these days.

This wasn't always the case. There was a time when Louise traveled with Barbara as a bass player. She accompanied her older sister on her first tour of Europe. She traveled the byways with the Do-Rites. She paid her own special kind of dues. It must have been tough for her, standing in the shadows watching her sister winning all the acclaim. Only lately has she become as aggressive as her older sister.

Take, for example, the leadership she exerted during the accident and its aftermath. She called many of the shots. She filled the stage for her sister. At some point she obviously decided to take charge. It seems that in her case, as in that of Irlene, she had become accustomed to letting someone else lead the way. Not any more. Louise now has her own booking agency; it happens to be the same one that books for Barbara, as well as for a dozen other top names.

Louise had a few problems of her own along the way. After one failed marriage, she virtually dropped out of sight for a few years. She was rumored to be estranged from the family. She had not been involved in music, and was eking out a living doing odd jobs in Texas.

Another go at marriage, this time to a Nashville musician, also failed. For Louise, the vaunted Mandrell charm didn't seem to be working. The subsequent illnesses of her mother and her father brought her home, seeking refuge, trying to find herself. Along came R. C. Bannon. A successful songwriter, he hooked up with Louise in 1979.

Their Las Vegas marriage seemed to rekindle Louise's interest in show business, and the two turned to making records along with maintaining a marriage. They recently adopted a three-year-old girl named Megan Nicole.

Louise likes to talk about the new addition to the Bannon family, and is often quoted in the press on the subject of her daughter. "She's been ours since last October [1986]. We had a year of normal lifestyle, but I am afraid she couldn't wait. Even before the adoption was final, she would say, 'Mommy, I got to work.' She couldn't wait to get on the stage. So now, sometimes, I let her come on stage and sing a song. Barbara had a surprise birthday party for Irlene last week, because on the twenty-eighth [Irlene's birthday] we will be working on the *Hollywood Squares* and here comes Nicole to talk about her. She said she was just going to be a mommy just like her aunt Irlene someday. . . . God knew what He was doing when He put her with us."

Louise has done a steady stream of commercials and is the spokesperson for several leading products today. She has had four hit singles. Away from Barbara's shadow, she seems to be flourishing. Her hits include "Band of Gold" (1979–Epic), "I Never Loved Anyone Like I Loved You" (1979–Epic), "Some of My Best Friends Are Old Songs" (1982–RCA) and "Save Me" (1982–RCA). She has also made two albums: *Louise Mandrell* (1981–Epic) and *Close-Up* (1982–RCA).

In 1981 Louise won accolades as she reached the same audience Barbara attracts. In that year alone, her awards included the *Music City News*'s Most Promising Female Vocalist and its TV Show of the Year; the Texas Legislature's Yellow Rose of Texas award and the Tennessee City Manager's "Tennessee Sweetheart" award. With her husband, she was nominated Top Vocal Group by the Academy of Country Music.

As collaborators, the talented pair have pushed the edges of the charts since they began performing together in 1979. The twosome's efforts include "I Thought You'd Never Ask" (1979–Epic), "Reunited" (1979–Epic) and "Our Wedding Band" (1982–RCA). They also have four duet

LP albums on the market. R. C. himself has over a dozen singles in circulation. The earliest came in 1977, two years before he married Louise. He also has two solo albums to his credit. The marriage has given exposure to him and stability to her. But there is much more to it than this. Judged by artistic criteria, they have a dynamic relationship.

What is the relationship between Barbara and her younger siblings? The three sisters claim to be best friends. They are neighbors. They work together. They play together. Until the for-sale signs went up a few years ago, Louise owned a house just down the road from Barbara on Old Hickory Lake. Irlene and her husband live just ten minutes away. (Mary and Irby live just a few miles up the way in Whitehouse, Tennessee.) When Louise throws a slumber party like the one Barbara described in a newsletter, it is easy for them to get together.

In a lengthy and wide-ranging March 1980 interview in *Glamour* magazine, the Mandrell sisters talked about their relationships.

Barbara said, "Playing professionally so young, I had responsibilities other kids that age didn't. Louise is like my right arm. I'm her biggest fan and vice versa. . . . I like to think I'm the thoughtful one, but it's Louise that surprises you with gifts for no reason. Irlene is really dingy, but not in a stupid way. She kids around, always putting you on. We each have our own thing; there's no reason to be jealous."

Louise commented, "The reason we get along so well is our years of practice. I credit our parents. We weren't allowed to argue. When we did, we were punished. Not one, but two or all three of us, so we'd pull together."

Irlene, the youngest, stated, "I don't know how most younger sisters are treated by their older sisters, but I get babied. . . . I like being the youngest and I wouldn't trade. They take care of me and I need it. There is no future in drums for a girl."

If the *Glamour* interview makes the sisters sound like cheerleaders for one another, that may not be far from the truth. Louise observed, with considerable enthusiasm, "We're proud of each other. . . . If you ever once ask me one question about Barbara, I'm going to do a half hour of it. But the one thing that upsets me is when people don't believe I'm me. I'm not Barbara."

Louise is the free spirit of the trio, but she has a sensitive, sentimental side as well. In addition to performing, she also writes poetry and songs. She has published a book about the family, *The Mandrell Family Album,* which celebrates the family success story.

She first thought about writing the book when she had been doing her first TV show with Barbara for a number of years. She became very sentimental. She started reminiscing, and her recollections made Barbara quite emotional. The oldest of the three sisters was in tears before she went out on stage that night.

Louise gave brief vignettes of herself and her family in *The Mandrell Family Album.* She says of Barbara: "She stretches herself to the limit." Of Irlene, she observes: "She was probably the biggest challenge for my folks because they never knew if she was serious or not."

Irlene, the youngest Mandrell daughter and the only nonsinger among the sisters, was the recipient of much attention from her older siblings.

She is the most elusive of the trio. She doesn't seem nearly as motivated to compete as the other sisters. She had a brief rise to the top, then seemed to drop out of sight in recent years.

In July of 1986, Irlene was nominated for an award as

Best Comedian of a TV series by *Music City News* for her regular contribution to the *Hee-Haw* series. She has seemingly found her niche in the perennial country variety series, convincingly playing the Cornfield County telephone operator. Often described as slightly dizzy, off-the-wall, Irlene does comedy best. She has also added to her list of credits several appearances on *Love Boat*. Recently she entered the home-video market with a tape that features a "Texas country" flavor and also opened her own museum in Pigeon Forge, Tennessee. It is similar to Barbara's, and located near Dollywood, USA, Dolly Parton's new theme park at the foot of the Smoky Mountains. Although the purpose of the Mandrell museums is similar, they don't compete for the same audience, since Pigeon Forge is several hundred miles east of Nashville.

Irlene's husband is Ric Boyer, a photographer and singer. He is more popularly known as the bass player for Eddie Rabbit's band. They recently added to the ever-expanding Mandrell clan when Irlene gave birth to Derric in December of 1986.

Despite the abundance of family feeling, three women from the same family and in the same occupation inevitably come into occasional competition. It has not always been smooth sailing. Some friction is unavoidable, since comparisons will be drawn by critics and other outsiders. At one point earlier in her career, Louise was reeling from the fact that her first two albums had died on the charts. Barbara was being lauded at a time when she herself seemed to be on slippery ground. It took some effort to deal with the disparity. Louise said in that unfortunate period, "I remind myself that Barbara is five years older than me—which means I have some time to catch up."

Louise, in 1986 and 1987, has begun appearing frequently on the networks. Aggressive new career management is allowing her to break new ground. With appearances on *Hammer, Hee-Haw,* and *Hollywood Squares* (with Irlene), the *Tonight Show, Lifestyles of the Rich and Famous, Love Boat, Fame* and *Crazy Like a Fox*—just to name a few of the most successful prime-time shows—Louise is gaining acclaim both as a comedienne and as a serious actress.

She has admitted to being nervous about seeing herself for the first time on the air in a dramatic role. "I was terrified. For some reason I am more nervous now than when we did it. There was the confusion of going back and forth."

As to her musical career, where there is more direct competition with Barbara, Louise is doing well. Barbara has been supportive, and even goes out of her way to lend encouragement.

Despite the hype and the constant buzz of publicity that surrounds them, that in some way makes their continued existence possible, most superstars are committed to their seclusion. Even in America, home of superstars and celebrities, people need a family life and a place away from the crowd. Celebrities less vocal than Barbara in their support of family values feel the need for a place to be together with husbands or wives, with children and parents. Barbara and Ken are more adamant than many show-business couples about their need to be with each other and even their family.

The Dudney home rests on five acres along the waterfront. It sits back from the road, a fortress. (Her property also features a horse barn across Windsor Drive, the now-famous street where she has lived.) For all her willingness to be with her fans, this is Barbara's last refuge. A high wall and shrubs obscure the view. All that can be seen from the front is a few cars, sometimes her Chevy Suburban. A security system notifies the nearest police of intruders. The place is some twenty-five miles from downtown Nashville, reached by a maze of twisting, turning, poorly paved roads. The turn into the subdivision seems ordinary enough. It might be any out-of-the-way, upper-middle-class neighborhood in the USA. The crucial difference is the steady stream of tour buses and fan-loads of vehicles snaking along the country way.

Although the home itself is secluded, explicit directions are posted by various businesses in the nearby town. The gift shop at nearby Twitty City gives directions for several of the stars' homes. This, of course, is singer Conway Twitty's contribution to Nashville tourism. It is a complex of gift shops and performance halls, a must-see for die-hard country music fans.

All this ruckus causes a strain on the locals. Traffic is snarled from summer to fall. Tourist buses lumber by. Necks turn to gawk at the Mandrells' residences. But there is little resentment among the neighbors. A nearby strip of asphalt now even carries the singer's name. A portion of Gallatin Road was renamed in honor of Barbara a few years ago.

In mid–1986, the local press reported that both Barbara and Louise were quietly trying to sell their homes on Old Hickory Lake. News articles stated an asking price for Barbara's home of $1.3 million; Louise's was around $975,000. Barbara's desire to sell stemmed from the constant stream of tourists to her residence.

Buddy Payne is Barbara's former bookkeeper turned realtor. The obvious question was whether or not Barbara or Ken would be present when the house was shown to potential buyers. This could mean that a serious fan might pose as an interested purchaser just to get to the singer.

Buyers would be carefully screened. There were a few so far who had actually toured the place. Buddy has said, "To my knowledge none of the other agents have shown it. We've only shown it three times."

Barbara has reportedly purchased a 100-acre tract near Goodlettsville, where she plans to build the house of her dreams. State Representative Ray Clark confirmed that the entertainer had purchased a tract near Joelton on White's Creek in Davidson County.

Her mother, Mary, told the press that Barbara has always had a longing for a more rustic home. "She's always wanted a log cabin and preaches to me about them all the time. They built one for Ken's grandmother and Barbara has wanted one ever since." Mary added the singer would not be leaving the Nashville area. "This is my home," Barbara had said.

The Mandrells were faced with an increasing deluge of traffic due to the inability of their attorneys to limit commercial activity on the narrow country pikes. They cited tour buses "from up North" as a problem. A proposed bill to limit tour buses was ruled unconstitutional. It would also have complicated the use of any heavy trucks, including dump trucks and even school buses.

The singer and her family have made a living from their high public profile. Barbara's image as a star accessible to her fans pervades the entire organization. Even her sisters have adopted the strategy. The extended family openly courts the fans while on tour. With autographs and smiles, the Mandrells continue to pay homage to the folks who boosted them to the top. It is still their public attitude. On tour, they stick to the practice, but with limited access that seems to grow smaller and smaller as the years go by.

The increasing need for privacy is quite defensible as their popularity grows, but this very fact only serves to increase their distance from the fans they serve. The insulation is necessary in their industry, but this is ultimately a self-defeating strategy.

In terms of approachability, the best advice for the dedicated fan is this: Buy a ticket, buy a spray of roses, go to a concert featuring the Mandrells (any combination of them). During the concert walk to the front of the stage. Give the flowers to the Mandrell of your choice. Ask for an autograph.

As cold and calculated as this approach may seem, it beats the other method: Buy a ticket on a tour bus or van, which they now have employed, or get directions from a Hendersonville native. Cruise the maze of rural lanes across the pastures to Windsor Drive in subdivision number one in Hendersonville. Slowly drive by the white wrought-iron main gate. Get out. Peer in, look around. That's it.

You'll have better luck at a concert filled with thousands of screaming fans.

8

The Person Behind the Performer

IN NOVEMBER OF 1982, Barbara had a lengthy conversation with Don Cusie about her impact in the music world, and its related influence on the Christian music scene. The interview was published in *Contemporary Christian Music Magazine*.

She began by placing herself clearly in perspective. "I am not some brilliant, philosophical person. I am not trying to get great teaching through my music. I am trying to do just one thing and that is to entertain. . . . The gospel album is where I put my foot down and said 'This is an exception. I am making this album for me.' But with my other music I am simply trying to be a commercial success, and by being a commercial success I know that I am doing my job."

Most of her fans know that she is proud of her accomplishments, and of those of her family. In the interview, it became apparent that accomplishment in and of itself is something she prizes.

She has been criticized, for a variety of reasons, by numerous mainstream Christian groups over the years. While claiming to be from very conservative roots, she has pushed back the edge of acceptability with controversial song lyrics. Some of her more fervent fans have expressed the thought that she should go into full-time gospel music. She resists any such suggestion.

Barbara's sense of herself, and of her faith, is firmly rooted in the realities of the secular world. Her conversation with Cusie made it obvious that she is serious about the responsibility. But it also clarified her sense of priorities. There are satisfactions, not to mention rewards, available to secular performers that are not realistic expectations for the religious performer. For the moment, her more devout fans will have to be content with the gospel tune or two that are a regular feature at her concerts, which average nearly ten thousand people a show.

Perhaps it is because of the candor with which she discusses her faith, or maybe because there are so few sources of inspiration left in the modern world, that people look up to Barbara. She wants very much to deserve that trust. She knows, based on her fan mail, that she is something of a role model. It is a burden, but one she manages with a smile. Her good humor and firm sense of self allow her to be more natural for her audience than many more studied performers. If she can have an impact, and reinforce some positive values, it just might be that she is a greater force for good than any dozen zealots with long faces. And she manages it by being herself.

Barbara recognizes the need for a variety of musical forms. Like most of us, she herself has varied tastes. Different kinds of music provoke emotions in her, but with gospel music, she finds something extra. The music itself sometimes touches her more deeply than a good sermon with a powerful message. Why she responds is a mystery to her. She doesn't know whether it is a function of age, maturity or something else entirely.

Barbara's faith is as much a quest as it is a dogmatic shield. The more she learns, the more she wants to know, and that knowledge encourages her to grow. She and Ken socialize with her minister and his wife and very often the topic under discussion has nothing to do with music or Christianity. She believes that a good Christian need not spend every spare moment talking about religion.

The interview in *Contemporary Christian Music Magazine* also addressed the bottom line for many of the southern fundamentalists who follow her: Is she a "born-again" Christian? She replied, "Yes, I was very young. I believe I was ten. . . . There was a visiting missionary in the church talking to all of us, and he started talking about the crucifixion and why Christ died for us. Then he said, 'What are you going to do for Him?' It just really hit for the first time what it was all about."

She admits a strong dislike for denominations. She has been to Methodist, Episcopal, Catholic, Baptist and Presbyterian churches. Raised Pentecostal, she was married in a Presbyterian church. For Barbara, denominations are almost beside the point. What matters is that the faith itself be for real—a church where the worshippers put God first instead of doctrine, or buildings and offerings. She currently attends Hendersonville Chapel, and feels lucky to have a church that conforms to her strong sense of what religion should be.

Despite the passion with which she adheres to her beliefs, she is tolerant of other opinions, perhaps to a fault, some of her critics suggest. She doesn't make it a practice to get "preachy" in her concerts, and she has good reasons. A primary consideration is that it's very bad business. She also has enough humility to question whether she has the right to tell others what they ought to think or do. She extends this reluctance to matters of politics and conscience. She knows that voting is important, and she exercises that right for herself. Barbara has a right to her opinions, and admits that some might find her opinionated, but she would never impose her ideas on other people. Despite her personal practices, however, she refuses to be judgmental of other entertainers who feel differently, and are willing to discuss, even to campaign for, their political and social agendas. If they want to speak out, that's fine with Barbara.

Mandrell talked further about her faith in the charismatic magazine *Virtue:* "Every day I fall short and I'm not what God wants me to be, but He loves me enough to let me try again and to forgive me. I know me and I'm not a person for everyone to pattern their lives after."

She told *Virtue* that she prays often, and that her approach is utilitarian, touching on personal and career matters, as well as more ethereal concerns. One example of Barbara's daily use of career-oriented prayer involves an incident that took place at the Washington State Fair, near the end of a three-month tour. She was hoarse. She routinely ended her concerts with a show-stopper—this time "The Battle Hymn of the Republic." "I knew I wasn't going to be able to hit the ending and I just said, 'Please, Jesus, give it to me.' I just laid back and the notes came! Maybe that's not a big miracle, that's everyday in my life, but it's important to turn to Him."

Barbara quit her TV show, it has been rumored, because she was being pressured to compromise her Christian beliefs and values. Emphatically denying the rumors to *Virtue,* she stated: "I never compromised my principles. I was doing fourteen- to sixteen-hour work days and they were taking their toll. . . . I pulled out of the show because I am not willing to do anything in life half-way.''

She characterizes the show as the single most educational thing she has ever done. Since it was a true variety show, she was called on to do almost everything—from comedy skits to dancing to writing. It was a real challenge for her, but it was rewarding, too.

Barbara's band, the Do-Rites, are all Christians. She treats the seven musicians almost as part of the Mandrell clan. ''My band is my musical family. We're such buddies. . . . I can't say we set up Bible studies, but many times that's the topic of discussion. Maybe that's why you don't hear a lot of harsh words and bickering. Everybody loves everybody.''

Organizing a Bible study group someday is high on her priority list. She brings to the notion the same enthusiasm she brings to the stage. She told the *Virtue* interviewer: ''It's like reading a novel; I don't want to put it down. I read it until I fall asleep at night. I've dog-eared it, but I've liked this Bible so much that I'm going to go through it again and start marking it with different colored pens.''

She has also taken a lot of flak for her repertoire, particularly from the more conservative segments of her audience. This is hardly surprising, since blues and honky-tonk music have long been vilified as ''the devil's music'' by the vociferously God-fearing Southerner. Barbara understands the objection, but takes a broader view of her role.

But, as resistant as she might be to complaints from true believers, she is as insistent that the full spectrum of country music, both secular and devotional, be represented in her act, regardless of where she might play. ''I'm planning on an appearance in Las Vegas. I'll be doing one hour and fifty minutes on stage. I'm taking dancers and my musicians, and I'm taking a gospel group from Nashville. I'm going to do a gospel segment in Vegas,'' she said in an interview.

Her father and she have been very close over the years. Barbara sometimes wonders if they are too close. Like any daughter who is close to her father, she can't imagine a time when she won't have him. This is something that has been especially important to her lately, since Irby recently suffered a serious heart attack. Bypass surgery corrected the problem, but the intimation of mortality was not lost on her.

She was subdued as she recalled the anxiety of that period in her interview with *Virtue:* ''I know the Lord promises we would never have something that we couldn't bear. I was never exposed to death until recent years. And when you have gone through your whole life and you are thirty-three years old and never had to deal with that, it is pretty tough.''

To some people, that kind of trust seems excessively naive, to others downright silly. But Barbara is neither naive nor silly. Her passion redeems her pronouncements on religion, and the obvious sincerity with which she delivers them springs from deep within her. Her beliefs sustain her in a harsh, even brutal, business. The rollercoaster life of musical performance can run the gamut from extreme exhilaration to abject discouragement.

Like any performer, she has ups and downs to cope with. When she comes off the stage after a performance, she is on a high like none that can be described unless you have experienced it. To have that sort of love affair with so many people at one time is overwhelming and emotionally draining. But, inevitably, she has to come down. The feeling then is akin to depression and can even be devastating.

The pressure of a show business career is enormous, and Barbara has admitted that she sometimes cries and at other times feels like a time bomb. Some performers turn to drugs and alcohol. She has chosen another route, and turned to God.

Another potential problem has confronted her as she attempts to broaden her horizons. Her recent acting career might require that she play characters whose lifestyles are in conflict with her beliefs. She does not seem overly concerned, and told one interviewer with her usual common sense, "Don't you think it would kind of depend on the part? Wouldn't it depend on what happened to her or how it ended? God loves all of us. He loves prostitutes, too. And as Christians we're supposed to love them and pray for them. . . . It's like, I've recorded a lot of cheating songs, but there have been a lot of cheating songs I have turned down. It depends on the lyrics. What effect does it have on me? Is it real? I can't make a snap judgment. If you described a dress to me, I couldn't say I loved it unless I saw it."

But, despite her confident demeanor, she seems slightly defensive on the subject. She is wont to shy away from any sort of public controversy. Since it tends to polarize opinion, religion is a sore spot for her. Her willingness to recognize a broader spectrum of opinion than many of her fellow fundamentalists has provoked some negative comment. Her song choices over the years have caused some of her more conservative fans to feel as if she were not true to the Christian faith.

Barbara's home is, after all, Tennessee, the heart of the Bible Belt. The roots of fundamental beliefs grow deep here. Tennessee is a hot-bed of Christian conservatism and of Christian values, claiming to embody the mainstream American ethic. The Scopes trial is not old news here. Agrarian people dot the landscape. They are the backbone of Barbara's legions of fans.

Her Pentecostal roots also come from the region. This contributes to her sense of orthodoxy. Her roots temper the way she relates to family and work as an expression of her inner philosophy.

Mention the word "Pentecostal" to anyone in this region and you either provoke an argument or elicit many stereotypical images. It is strange that Barbara celebrates this aspect of her heritage, since she tends publicly to avoid anything that might even remotely generate strong opinions. This is not to suggest that she is apologetic about her faith—simply that she is aware that broad-mindedness is not a principal character trait of most fundamentalists. Barbara is nothing if not prudent.

The pioneer spirit is another tradition the area draws upon. Barbara values those traditions. She herself is a pioneer of sorts. She lives among the monuments of those who risked everything to settle here during the early days of the Republic and honed their rugged skills to survive. Self-sufficiency and individualism are the twin cornerstones of a work ethic born of their agricultural lifestyle. For such people, tolerance was a luxury they could ill afford.

Nashville, the state capital, was considered a rugged frontier outpost during the days when Tennessee's most famous son reigned in Washington. Andrew Jackson's Hermitage is only a few miles from the Mandrell homesite. The legendary Jim Bowie and Davy Crockett were notable among the state's early inhabitants. Some of the attributes of these frontier people are reflected in the current natives, and Barbara of course counts herself among them.

The Natchez Trace crosses just south of the state's second largest city. This pioneer route took settlers from the river port of New Orleans back to Tennessee's heartland.

The Civil War brought bloodshed and division to the soil and its citizens. The battles of Shiloh and Chickamauga Creek symbolized clashes between two ideologies. Some of the attitudes that divided the people of that time are still held by residents living in isolated pockets of Tennessee.

The state didn't really prosper as a part of the Industrial Revolution until the twentieth century. When the railroad helped open the land to settlement, Tennessee either became a jumping-off place for those on the way to the western prairies or the final destination for some who chose not to explore the farther limits of a country on the move.

It is from this heritage that the Mandrells originated. The conservative ethic that flourished here one hundred years ago is still strongly entrenched. It pervades Barbara's work and thought. The engaging performer can't stand to be idle; she must always be doing something.

Her faith has continually brought her through the fire. At the Fan Fair the summer following her accident, two thousand fans held hands and prayed for her. They thanked God for sparing her life, and prayed for her baby due in the fall.

But despite the contradictions in the woman herself, and in her audience, her successes come in all shapes and sizes and forms. In 1983 she was named one of the Top Style Makers of the Year by the National Hairdressers and Cosmetologists Association. She passed it off, instead of wallowing in the praise, giving credit to her hairdresser, Rahn McDow.

She flies him to whatever city she may be working. She calls him a "genius with color."

"When I first went to him, my hair was terribly damaged and not healthy. Between electric rollers and a blow-dryer about three times a day, my hair had taken a lot of abuse."

It is one of the striking paradoxes of country music that, while it celebrates simplicity and sings the praises of the ordinary life and the common man, its principal performers are often worlds away from their strongest fans. In the early days, consistent with the "down-home" roots of the music, Barbara had bragged about doing her own hair. That was something her fans could relate to, even respect. Now, more confident of their affection, she's enlisted Rahn's services to keep her appearance consistent. It gave her confidence and an emotional boost.

McDow runs a business called Creative Input Agency. He says of Mandrell, "Her hospitality still prevails." He has added blonde and brown highlights that improve on the original. She came to the award-winning stylist with hair he described as "shorter and sweeter. We wanted to try and change her image, so we let her hair grow longer to create a sexier look."

Mandrell has been listed as one of Mr. Blackwell's Worst Dressed Women. McDow felt that the general problem with women country music performers was too much hair. "It's never controlled and it never goes with the clothes."

Barbara prefers simplicity in dress and style. She's still a tomboy at heart. Every June close to twenty thousand country music fans converge on the city of Nashville for Fan Fair. It's a business convention in part, and the record companies put on shows of their various artists for the fans. But the event that opens the Fan Fair is a softball tournament. Barbara has a men's team and a women's team, and plays on the latter. Later in the summer, she and Conway Twitty have teams that play an exhibition game in Tennessee to raise money for the Humane Society there.

Barbara is an intense competitor, who can catch anything the men throw at her. She plays catcher, and when the opposing team is trying to score a run, she will not give any ground at the plate. She's an indifferent hitter but a good runner. And when you hit like she does, speed is important.

Her husband acknowledges her intense love of softball. According to him, she's a great catcher and fielder, and "she really likes being the catcher because that's where the action is."

Along with the Do-Rites, Barbara and Ken have taken home softball trophies on more than one occasion. Usually they play as a regular feature of Fan Fair. But she has spun her athletic ability into a gold mine for the sake of helping others through benefits. She has played the Kenny Rogers Celebrity Softball Benefit Tournament in Las Vegas. She has also held her own charity benefit games, including several to raise contributions to the Nashville Children's Hospital.

She has explained her dedication this way: "I only hope we can do some good. I did the Children's Hospital telethon and wasn't pleased at all with the money raised. Their need is so great, it was a tremendous frustration. That's why I started thinking about doing the games for the hospital. All the work will be worthwhile if we can raise a decent amount of money. I really feel that if the people are made aware of the game and its cause, they'll turn out."

One such Mandrell game drew twenty thousand fans to Greer Stadium in Nashville. Many noted celebrities show up on these occasions. In the past, Barbara has talked about the project with enthusiasm, and especially about the support from the famous. Despite her own success, she sounded like a star watcher herself on one occasion: "Brooke Shields—she's really a terrific gal. She wasn't with us last year, but her soft spot is children, and most of her charity work is for children. I met her a few years ago when Ken and I attended the first People's Choice Awards. We were sitting at the same table and struck up a great liking for each other. The next year, we were seated at the same table again. The next time we saw each other was when she and Michael Jackson were sitting in front of us at the American Music Awards."

Among the other celebrities who have appeared at Barbara's games are Morgan Fairchild, David Hasselhoff, Patrick Duffy, Minnie Pearl, Roy Acuff, Gladys Knight, Bill Anderson, Dottie West, Sylvia, Marie Osmond, Lee Greenwood, Ralph Emery, Bobby Wright, Little Jimmy Dickens, Vince Ferragamo, David Frizzell, Harry Reasoner and Dave Rowland.

Louise and Irlene, along with Nashville's mayor, also participate, as do the kiddy characters Winnie the Pooh, Goofy, Pluto, and Mickey and Minnie Mouse. The effort is a continuing success. In one game in 1984, Patrick Duffy's team—the Hotshots—beat the Do-Rites 8–7, and over $100,000 was raised for the Vanderbilt Children's Hospital.

Barbara stated in fun before the game, "Patrick seems to be pretty fired up and making a lot of threats about tearing me up on the field." She was planning to send Ferragamo along with Walter Payton to counterbalance her opponents. "And I'll send Irlene, Morgan and Brooke up to bat and those guys on the field won't be able to pay any attention to the ball." A good time was had by all.

Mandrell's benevolent spirit is not confined solely to

softball. Nor solely to Nashville. Every year in October, she holds a benefit golf tournament in Birmingham, Alabama. Originating in Montgomery, it moved to the southern steel capital to raise money for the Alabama Sheriff's Boys' and Girls' Ranches. The Statler Brothers and Wayne Newton are among the celebrities who have participated in recent years. The tournament is held at the Green Valley Country Club and raises nearly $500,000 annually. The highlight of the weekend usually includes a benefit concert with Barbara, Louise and R. C. Bannon headlining the event.

The Ranches are located in Stillwater, Alabama. They serve one hundred seventy neglected, abandoned or abused children. They do not receive any government money, and are entirely funded by charity efforts like this one, upon which they are dependent for continued operation.

Close scrutiny of the personal dimension of Barbara Mandrell reveals evidence of the genuine human warmth she possesses. She is in a position to use her influence not just to claim awards, not just to be successful, but to help others. And unlike so many others who have that same influence, she uses it.

A humanitarian who is also a .38 sharpshooter, a singer who has flown with the Thunderbirds, the Navy's flying acrobats—there seems to be no end to Barbara's abilities or to her daring spirit. She loves the chance to show other dimensions of her personality.

"I'm ready to get in my jeans right now. I love them. I think I get a different attitude when I'm all dressed up. When I have a skirt on, not only out of being a lady and being modest, I find I sit differently, walk differently, and the clothes give me that attitude. It's like that beautiful old song, 'I Feel Pretty.' "

Yet the contrasts and contradictions within her seem to

endear her to the fans rather than to alienate them. What might seem hypocritical in a less appealing performer is, in Barbara's case, simply an exercise of the fundamental right to be inconsistent. "I've enjoyed, especially when I've been out to California, having a manicurist come to my home, and I get a manicure once a week. That's the biggest treat I've ever had. Maybe I'd had five in my whole life [before the show]. And when someone plays string instruments the way I do, you can't have nice hands. With this treat, I look and feel as if I have someone else's hands in front of me."

Like all of us, she likes variety. She explained: "I love to go without makeup or combing my hair. Not because I think it's good for my hair or for my face, but because I'm lazy. I do five shows a week, and I'm pooped by the weekend. So I save that time for the kids and Ken. I look like an old hag and I love every minute of it.

"My hairdresser, Rahn, doesn't allow me to have a permanent, so we decided to have my hair 'woven.' " (This is a process in which blonde highlights are "woven" into her natural brown.)

Her record company hired a makeup artist to work with her, Bobby Joe. "He is the first person and only person I've ever let totally strip my face and do it for me." She said of her soft, false eyelashes, "I even wear them to the grocery store."

How does she stay beautiful while on the road? She's got some new accessories built into her room on her newest (third) bus. Irby, Ken and Barbara designed the inside of the bus, and used their extensive touring experience to great advantage. She has an elaborate makeup room that even lets her see the back of her head.

What about her weight? How does she maintain the petite figure? She is certainly active, but it is her eating habits that have the greatest impact. She admits that she rarely eats three meals a day except when she's on vacation.

Her appearance is, of course, important to her career, but a comment she made to one reporter suggests there's some friendly competition going on among the Mandrell sisters. "You know when you have a sister that looks like Louise you get an inferiority complex."

In an interview with Linda Luoma in March of 1979, yet another facet of her complex character emerges. Barbara told her, "I don't even like the word 'star.' It has the connotation of an 'I'm better than you' attitude. I think of myself as a performer or artist. I just happen to do what I do to make a living before the public, and that makes me well-known."

Her commitment to quality was present even back then. The most pervasive aspect of her character is the drive to excel, whether it be in athletic competition, on stage or in the studio. She wants, and probably even expects, that each single and album will be better than the last.

But it's also important to remember that she is human. She has flaws. She's real. It's easy to forget that. After all, she has such a regal bearing and polished exterior. Yet there are glimpses of the woman, even the little girl. Peek into her soul and you peek into a rather extraordinary personality, complete with neuroses. She has all the drives and motivations that power the average person toward his notion of success. The main difference is the level at which she operates.

She is an extremely successful executive, but still highly insecure. It's easy to speculate that she's afraid someday all this might end. Underneath the trappings of celebrity is a vulnerable person who still has the same needs as anyone else, a woman who suffers the same emotional ups and downs as the rest of us, but considerably intensified by the position of power she occupies.

It's a lonely place to be. She is unable to go out and be a regular person. Everything she says and does is recorded. Her opinions are evaluated by all and sundry, her every move scrutinized by press and public alike.

With it all, she has managed to construct a life to be envied. She is the perfect entertainer, and yet she maintains a touch of the ordinary. Her complicated personality allows her to be mother and wife by day, superstar by night. The TV star and award winner is also a charitable hostess with a heart as big as her bank accounts. It is hard to believe that Barbara Mandrell, never placing herself above others, is anything other than what she seems to be: just an example of the American dream and what it can bring if one has the essential ingredients and works hard enough.

9

Businesswoman

WHEN DOES IT quit being fun? When does the exercise of talent turn into a strain, the joy of performance become a chore? The talented singer recently was featured on TV in her "Get to the Heart" tour special. During that performance, barely discernible, was a glimpse of trouble. Perhaps detectable only by the most observant fan, or by the trained eye of a critic, it was nevertheless there. It ran through all her show-biz happy talk, her list of oldie tunes and antics with the boys in the band. What was it? *Boredom*.

Although present only in faint traces, it was there. The tired look of running down the old stuff, watching the audience bringing down flowers and gifts. They were involved but Barbara seemed detached and remote.

For the most part, she gave it her best. She never turned in a lousy performance. The show itself was as good as always, just as slick and polished as ever. Her singing and musical skills were, if anything, more sharply honed. And her audience rapport is still second to none.

Yet, behind the eyes, the tired, worn-out look shone through. Barbara was running it down just one more time. It was so effortless for her. There was no challenge. It was too easy. Challenge has been the lifeblood of her career, her response to it the source of her success. Just doing a simple concert seemed elementary now. She acted so nonchalant. The electricity was absent, the edge was gone. In its place was a truly good act, but the undercurrent of boredom was a reminder that the glitter can fade. For any entertainer who wants to avoid this trap, new interests have to be developed, new goals have to be set.

There are many reasons why Barbara continues in the touring trap. Possibly she feels obligated to continue to do concerts. Or, maybe she feels that this is the only thing she can do well. So she returns night after night to prove something to herself, that she can still do it, that she can get the old thrill back one more time. She has to prove that she can still cut it with the fans and with herself.

Her mood is easy to misread. Whatever the apparent malaise may be, boredom may not be a completely fair assessment. It could signify the presence of a truly deep and abiding relationship with the audience, like that of a married couple. They know her. She knows them. No frills are necessary. They need no pretense. She can get right to the songs and do them. There is no need for a lot of fancy stuff. Everyone is on the same wavelength.

Any suggestion that Barbara felt "ho-hum" about the performance might be explained away by saying that this was not a representative performance. This was just a bad night for an otherwise notable performer.

Mandrell Productions would certainly never put anything on that seemed to her less than perfection. That is, unless they weren't aware of it. They might not have the objectivity to really see that she is going through the motions—she's really giving it to them, singing her lungs out, not missing a beat—but it's a lackluster performance, without any excitement other than that of hearing favorite old songs.

The Mandrells are certainly not strangers to business. Entrepreneurial instincts have helped put Barbara where she is. It takes more than musical talent to become rich, famous and successful. It takes thoughtful management, shrewd development of a product that is marketable. And the most critical aspect of all this is the ability to convince the public they need the product. MBA's learn all about creating brand awareness. The show-business equivalent is image. Packaging and marketing are the principal strategic concerns of American business. They are the guarantors of repeat sales. The Mandrells have made a mint putting such business principles into practice. They could write a text on the subject.

Diversification was a catch phrase in the marketplace in the seventies. Investment became a complicated game involving calculated risk based on good market research. That was also the theory behind the Barbara Mandrell Country Museum. It represented a risk, although Barbara herself never stopped to think whether it would be anything other than successful. That's another important principle of good sales: total belief in the product.

Barbara Mandrell Country is, first and foremost, a commercial enterprise. The concept is not exactly original. Other country music celebrities have similar operations— Johnny Cash, Hank Williams, Jr., Minnie Pearl, Waylon Jennings.

Yet Barbara's "non-museum," as she puts it, is genuinely different. She is tremendously enthusiastic when she talks about it. On one occasion, she characterized it as the most emotional thing she's ever done in her life.

The building includes 15,000 square feet of display space. It features everything from childhood treasures and family heirlooms to a wide array of memorabilia that traces her career from the early days right up through the present.

There are five music-video presentations in the museum that use Mary's voice over a montage of old photographs. Mrs. Mandrell then tells a story as only a mother can. Also included on the videos are clips from *Town Hall Party,* old home movies and a range of appearances and activities from Barbara's early days.

She also has relics from her NBC series. She utilizes everything to make her point. Three director's chairs that were on the set of the show are in the museum. The clip begins with Barbara talking quietly, sitting in a chair. Then it zips through some of the clips in a series of fast edits—a pie in the face, coal falling on her head, Barbara in pratfall—lots of slapstick. There's also a sports video, which continues the comedy.

The video tour of the inside of the Mandrell home is one of the highlights. It is not just Barbara moving from room to room pointing to furniture. She was more interested in providing an entertaining display, one that was informed by her willingness to share intimacies with her fans. Occasionally she talks to the camera; at other times she is there only in voice-over, while the viewer eavesdrops on Barbara and her family. There is a sense of continuity to the exhibits that is sometimes eerie. At one point on the screen you watch Barbara packing up things from her trophy room. When you look left, there it is: the entire trophy room—carpet, light fixtures, drapes, furniture and many of Barbara's numerous awards—right in front of you.

This kind of exhibit would seem to draw a certain element, a special kind of fan, to the tour spot. It would also seem to appeal to a wide range of voyeurs who get their thrills by looking at Barbara's intimate belongings.

Barbara has gone to great lengths to re-create her house in Hendersonville. She once explained it this way: "There's a little tiny area—a small room—where I went in and painted the same mural that I painted on Jaime's wall when I was expecting her: of Winnie the Pooh. And then the things that I, as a mother, treasure: things of my children's . . . I have a lot of . . . things from fans in there that have been made [by the fans] and are unusual. For example, a gentleman that has been a fan of mine for a long time and is a master craftsman. He made me a long rifle. It's gorgeous. . . . and many lovely things that are handmade."

There are many other things that have personal significance. Barbara is not only a performer, she is also a country music fan, and the exhibit includes gifts from friends who are celebrities in their own right: Jimmy Dickens's guitar, one of Roy Acuff's fiddles, several things from Merle Travis. Half a dozen Hall of Famers are represented. In addition to those already mentioned, Minnie Pearl, Kitty Wells and Dolly Parton are there. She even has Sonny James's favorite fishing lures on display.

Barbara didn't want this to be a "museum" because she is in the middle of a very active career. Instead, she wanted it to be a friendly place to visit that provides an intimate look at her life. It certainly is that.

The concept is ordered and logical. She once explained the elaborate preparations for the collection: "We started accumulating the things and having them numbered and photographed. And I sat down and talked about each one. By the way, when you read about an item on the little plaque in the museum, it's all in my own words."

When someone asked why she has chosen to expose herself so totally, she said she did it for the fans. "It's because we are so close. . . . I want to share those things, but of course it's impossible to bring people into my house. So we've dang near moved it all down there to Music Row.

"It's sure been an emotional thing. Ken saw the first examples of some of the displays that were being constructed, and he came home and I bet he talked to me for two hours about how impressed he was. It's done just beautifully. One other nice thing is the jobs we're generating. Everyone on the project, even the museum expert, is from Tennessee."

She acquired the property from CRC Equities, Inc., in 1984. In the lobby of the Country Music Association's building, she unveiled her plans in January of that year. The site is a stone's throw from her place on Division Street.

Originally, the building was occupied by Country Crossroads, a computer-animated, country-puppets extravaganza. A sing-along sound recording studio was also located on the premises. The concept was unsuccessful from the start, and Barbara took over the facility after the first entertainment enterprise failed. The land was originally purchased from the city. CRC spent $3.2 million developing the site. Another $300,000 in expenses was anticipated to get the place ready for Barbara's use.

"I've been approached many times about this sort of thing, but I never reacted 'til CRC came to me a few months ago with their proposal," said Mandrell. "The concept is really mine and I will have my little fingers on everything that goes in over there." With pride, she continued, "I want them to meet my pets, see where I cook and all those things."

The Mandrell exhibit is directly across the street from Nashville's Country Music Hall of Fame. The Hall's displays are exotic and cover a wide range of artifacts: Morgan Fairchild's stockings from *Flamingo Road;* Linda Carter's Wonder Woman bracelets; Tom T. Hall's hunting jacket and rifle.

The facility is located in a prime spot, on the sheer edge of the recording industry's backyard. Nearby, one can find the studio where Elvis cut some of his records and the headquarters of all the major labels. The area teems with magazines, writers and agents—all the support staff needed to run the multibillion-dollar-a-year business of Country Music.

The Mandrell museum souvenir program is written directly to the fan. It is designed to give the feeling that each passerby has shared an intimate moment with the star herself. She opens with a thank-you to the attending fans, and a promise of the good things to come. After the teaser, she gets right down to brass tacks.

She informs the visitor that Barbara Mandrell Country has been a longtime dream of hers. Making the dream a reality has been exciting work for her, as well as a labor of love. She compares the process of assembling the exhibit to wrapping the perfect gift for a loved one then having them wait until Christmas to open it. She says she has never been good at waiting, but now that the time has come she wants to be part of the celebration. In ecstatic prose, the brochure explains the significance each item has to Barbara.

The writing style is full of the same earnest sincerity one has learned to expect from the star. One might expect that either the fans really fall for this line or they get awfully sick from the "gingerbread." There is, however, a third option, and it seems to be the one most frequently chosen: They do neither. They go through the tour dutifully as if the hype is expected, par for the course. If they are turned off by its excess, the fans don't show it.

The facility is laid out in semicircular areas, each with a different theme or designation. The entrance opens into the ticket-purchase area, and after being admitted, the fan is led to an introductory display. This consists of a video containing a welcome greeting and explaining what to expect. The visitor then proceeds through the winding maze of cases to the next area, the Living Scrapbook Video. Barbara's first Rolls-Royce is passed on the left in the process. It is a red 1963 Silver Cloud. The Early Career Section is next. It is stocked with clippings and mementos from Barbara's early days. Her wedding gown hangs there as well.

At this point in the tour, several other video displays can be viewed. HBO segments, clips from the entertainer's series and other video snippets are presented. Her trophy room follows, immediately adjacent to an exact replica of her bedroom. A number of personal items share the space here. They include Mandrellesque elegies to family members and exhibits of family history. In one such, she talks about her Aunt Linda and Uncle Al. She tells the visitor that Louise and Irlene stayed with the couple during the Mandrell Family Band tours of Southeast Asia. Uncle Al, who was her father's oldest brother and a very talented jazz drummer, was the one who taught Irlene to play. Aunt Linda is represented by a crocheted bedspread she had made and given to Barbara. The spread hangs in the case behind.

Other memorabilia include a personally signed Burt Reynolds picture and a large color photograph inscribed to Barbara from Ronald Reagan. Praise for old friend Roy Clark joins that for Dottie West, one of her favorite gospel singers. Dottie performed on ''He Set My Life to Music,'' and the exhibit includes her first guitar, made by her brother aboard a ship during World War II.

There's more. In fact, sensory overload gets to be a problem. There is a lot crammed into each display. In one, Barbara tells how country singer Sylvia used to attend her recording sessions while still working as a secretary. Sylvia is now not only a recording artist in her own right, but a gifted visual artist. A picture she has done of Barbara is on display, and the likeness indicates the now-famous singer is a truly gifted artist.

Other treasures are more personal. One, explained in the exhibit itself, is typical of the degree of intimacy Barbara is willing to permit her fans.

"MTYLTT . . . More Than Yesterday Less Than Tomorrow." This is a private code Ken and she have used with each other. The exhibit explains that Ken began using the expression when he first sent flowers to Barbara. Now, anywhere in the world she could receive flowers with no other message and know they came from Ken. The risk, of course, in this kind of openness is that now anyone else, in or out of his right mind, could send flowers with that code. But this is the kind of risk Barbara is willing to take for the sake of the concept. In the exhibit, the initials are inscribed on a gold bracelet resting in a glass and chrome case.

A gold pendant with a diamond and gold cracker was a gift of the Cattle Baron's Ball in Texas. They immortalize the words to one of the legends in song, "You Can Eat Crackers in My Bed."

Then there's a piece of rock, an original chunk of stone from the Missouri State Penitentiary. It is inscribed:

HAPPY BIRTHDAY
BARBARA MANDRELL

''SHE WAS COUNTRY WHEN
COUNTRY WASN'T COOL.''
WE LOVE YOU
CONVICTS MISSOURI STATE
PENITENTIARY
1981 FROM ORIGINAL WALL 1873
WARDEN WYRICK   + 34092

The list is endless. She keeps adding and adding to the exhibit. She keeps on, with new displays, new comments and descriptions, in an effort to attract repeat business. And she does. The prospective clientele is endless, as tourists pour out from buses and the nearby shops and restaurants.

It is very convenient to line up at the ticket counter on a hot summer day. The steep admission price seems of no consequence; all are eager to taste the Music City experience. Ryman Auditorium has probably preceded this stop. The tourists' appetites have been whetted. Now they are ready for the Hall of Fame and, of course, Mandrell Country. This will be followed by a visit to the nearby Opryland facility, several miles away. The tour is capped off with a concert at the Opry itself. This undoubtedly is Country Music heaven, and Barbara is right in the thick of the action.

The pressure sometimes shows. ''Right now, it's kind of a tough time. You know, I don't mean to say it in a complaining way, because I'm so elated and grateful for all the things going on. But nevertheless, it's very hard to juggle so many things and try to do a good job with each.''

Barbara made this confession to a journalist, when she had just come off the road from a trip into Virginia.

"Normally, the road is a place to catch up on sleep, but lately, it's been my place to catch up on projects."

Barbara's projects are overseen by Ken, her business manager. Her talent and stage bookings are handled by an agent, JoAnn Berry, president of World Class Talent. World Class is a chic, stylish island surrounded by down-home entertainers. It seems like a tiny piece of the Big Apple set in the middle of Country Music USA. The offices are located a few doors from Mandrell Country. Rather obscure, they are identified only by a sign that hangs above the entrance. But once inside, one is impressed with the balance, the harmony. Ms. Berry is a cool, trendy professional. Her tastes in decor are superb. She masterfully applies all the tools of her demanding trade to the volatile environment she works in. Good marketing skills are essential to success in her field, and she knows her stuff. Like any sharp agent, she has a nonsense detector. She can distinguish those truly interested in booking her client for an engagement from those just trying to get close to the popular singer for an interview.

The talent-booking business is built on image and word of mouth. For JoAnn that word must be pretty good. She controls some of the hottest names in country: Bill Anderson, The Kendalls, Ronnie McDowell, Jeannie C. Riley, Johnny Rodriguez, Ricky Skaggs, Porter Wagoner, Freddy Weller, Penny DeHaven . . . and Barbara's sister Louise. Others, less well known but up-and-coming, also adorn the stables: Randy Travis, Robin Lee, Jim Glaser.

JoAnn's agency is a slick and polished outfit that knows the going rates. Barbara, at the present time, is listed at full retail: $70,000 for one performance. A negotiated reduction might be possible, but not likely. The posh decor of the agency reassures anyone who might be fearful of slipshod handling. The agency is strictly business, and has the firmest grasp of the still-growing commercial viability of country music. This is the home of the Fortune 500 of the country world.

The business savvy the Mandrells have developed is remarkable. Irby had kicked around in quite a few enterprises in his early days. He passed along to his oldest his sense of what would go and what wouldn't. Barbara, in turn, has parlayed her country skills into mass marketing success. The real secret, drawing in the fans as if they were partners, is a relatively little-used technique.

It is not a technique without risk, of course. There is the danger that it will create a false sense of kinship in some of the more devoted fans. They sometimes feel that she should be totally accessible, and disregard her right to a private life. Running into that invisible wall, as necessary as it might be, can lead to resentment.

While it is a touch risky, though, the benefits far outweigh the liabilities. The result has been the forging of a solid-as-iron identity between Barbara and her followers. She could sell them rags and they would line up to buy. It is not as cynical an approach as it might seem, however. There is considerable loyalty and genuine commitment on both sides. At least that's the way it appears. Barbara is dedicated to her fans' best interests, as long as they don't conflict with her own.

And she makes a whopping profit. All seventeen of her albums are still circulating. Her name is big in the country market and, thanks to her TV show, even beyond its borders. Barbara still gets considerable airplay. Even her oldies are moving into the category known as Country Classic.

How this process occurs is a mystery even to those in the business. Everyone knows the ingredients. First you must have a decent song to record. It must be something the broadest possible slice of the listening population can identify with. Then you must have a decent recording of the tune. The band has to be tight, the vocals precise and vibrant. The mixture has to be just right to catch the ear of the audience. Then you've got to have airplay, lots of airplay, and a favorable response from the DJs who control the airwaves. There has to be PR support and promotion by the record company. Crucial to the program is a blitz of magazine and TV exposure, personal interviews, anything to capture the public's attention. If you have all of the foregoing, and if you have the one indefinable catalyst, you have what everybody wants and nobody can predict: an inexplicable appeal that embraces all levels of the public.

The bona fide superstar is a much-discussed but still baffling phenomenon. The process by which a performer becomes a household word is the philosopher's stone of the talent-management business. Everybody knows a superstar when they see one. Elvis was one, and Sinatra before that. More recently, Springsteen and Madonna have attained superstardom. But when all is said and done, when all the ingredients have been anatomized and analyzed, all you can say for sure is that some performers create a peculiar reaction in the public while others don't. There are examples of performers who seem to have it all, and fizzle. They are missing the one mystical ingredient. No one knows what it is, but it is directly related to media and public approval on a gargantuan scale that borders on mass hysteria and obsession. Beatlemania is probably the paradigm. Whatever the magic might be, however, everyone agrees that superstardom comes only when these conditions are met.

It seems to boil down to the ability to strike a nerve in people at just the right time. The spontaneous combustion is further accelerated by unpredictable social currents that propel the potential superstar even higher. If you have it, the fans go wild. And if you don't, there is nothing you can do to get it. Where Mandrell falls on the spectrum is difficult to say. She is no Elvis, certainly, but she has an enormous following, fans who love everything she does and will travel thousands of miles to get a shot of it, like Theresa Smith.

At this point, hustling for interviews or appearances is unnecessary. They come in landslides. The rage is on and the performer goes along for the ride. The demands of the blitz can seem unbearable but, unfortunately, the public is also fickle.

It is possible to look back in old periodicals and rediscover a bevy of once up-and-coming superstars who have long been deleted from the national consciousness. Forgotten castoffs in a media landfill, discards heaped upon piles of hype, who never really had the substance, the staying power, the mystery ingredient without which a performer cannot withstand the erosion of time.

A changing public is full of whims and captured by trends that come and go full circle. This explains why forgotten legends often reappear years later. They come back more lined and graying. They are older and heavier, but whether they are wiser is open to debate. Once again they pull out the old stuff they used to do, this time for younger listeners to admire. And so it begins again.

The products of these performers keep turning up at out-of-the-way places. Isn't it interesting to browse through the bargain bin of a discount store or record shop? The labels are faded, the hits long forgotten. The public is given a substantial mark-down as an incentive to try them out. Some make the grade as bona fide collectibles and go on display at yard sales and in collector's fairs. They become legendary in value.

Many of the recordings are redistributed by specialty companies, which package them like strawberries at the supermarket. The 1-800 numbers flash. The announcer reads the details out in a singsong voice: "Original artists. Not available in any store!" The crawl line displays the titles as they are being sung by the artist. A number of tunes are strung together under a common theme, trying to appeal to a specific slice of the consumer market. And, incredibly, people buy.

All of this is to make a very important point about Barbara Mandrell. Note that she has been around a long, long time. She has endured the market whims. She has bridged the gaps of trends and changing times. She has remained viable over a long span, nearly thirty years, most of them on top, or at least on the upward slope. And there is no end in sight to her staying power. Barring any more major tragedy or scandal, she could make a lifetime of it.

It's true you can catch a few of her older efforts in the bargain bins. The pictures on the record jackets reflect dated fashions and hairstyles. Yet she is still there. And people know who she is. So they buy.

Maybe her fans are basically the same group who have stayed with her over the years. That was certainly true of Elvis and his devoted following. Both the King and his court were frozen in time. Barbara had said that most of her fans are women. Perhaps they see in her the beauty, talent and grace they lack. Maybe they are the families of the servicemen she entertained back when there was a war on. Maybe her fans are just part of a larger cadre of country music fans at large, who happen to specialize in Barbara Mandrell. No matter. She keeps on rocketing up the charts. Her appeal endures. The fans still pack the halls to see her, and she commands the price her agents ask for her.

For every performer, though, there is a cold, unblinking fear that accompanies every move, watches every step of the way. They wake up in a midnight sweat, knowing the merry-go-round may stop. The source may dry up. Although Barbara has not acknowledged that fear publicly, she cannot be immune to it. She may one day find herself deserted and without a fan to buy her records. Yet as emotionally awful as that would be, she is permanently assured of financial solvency.

She has an uncanny knack for keeping ahead of the game. The residuals from her prolific recording career should keep her afloat for a long while. The reservoir of revenues from the museum doesn't seem to be showing any signs of drought. She has had the foresight to keep changing things around and to put enough pizzazz in it to keep it alive. There is no reason to believe the future will be bleak.

Her television series could pop back up again. It could be passed off in syndication and make it like *Hee-Haw* has. Or it could turn up cannibalized. The sketches could be excised from the main body and stitched together to form a *Mandrell Sisters Comedy Club* show. Or her gospel songs could all be edited together to make for a really nifty religious program. She could put all her talking segments about religion together and might make it as a TV evangelist. It's time for a woman to give it a shot on the tube in this area. Who knows? But as long as there are creative marketing consultants, Barbara will survive.

She will also have Ken around. Even now, while she works the stage, he is often away, looking for investment opportunities, setting up new business deals, serving as her executive producer in many non-show-business ventures. For example, about five years ago, Ken was the prime mover behind a concept new to the southeastern United

States. He had spent some time in California while his wife worked on her series and had observed a number of one-hour photo processing labs while in LA. They piqued his curiosity, but he was busy with other projects. He filed the idea away for future consideration. A few months later, he returned to California and discovered that the first few shops had flourished and that the number of such businesses had grown dramatically. He saw dozens of them on street corners and in shopping centers. Convinced this was a trend of the future, he and another businessman, Tim Bucek, put together the capital to bring the concept to Tennessee.

In a former gas station near Rivergate Mall in Gallatin, the first Barbara Mandrell's One-Hour Photo Center began operations in early 1982. It is located on the same strip of highway where her accident took place two years later.

Its success was apparent from the beginning, and a second shop soon opened right down the street from the building where her museum would later be located. The couple has been working on franchising and expansion in various places across the country.

Ken said in April of 1982, ''We will probably end up with six in Nashville of our own, but we have a franchise organization in the works with our attorneys now. We're the first in Nashville and we'll be franchising across the nation.''

Start-up costs for the labs and retailer complex were in the neighborhood of $150,000, which does not include the cost of property. Actually, that is not bad for a high-tech retail enterprise these days.

Ken talked about the actual process. ''The film processing equipment is computerized and you can go in and actually watch your film being processed. The process is a high-quality one whose technology had been perfected before we went into the business. We're not going into this just to go out and make a dollar. Because Barbara's name is attached, we want our product to be a quality product. We'll be selling Barbara Mandrell's name.''

The shop is adjacent to World Class Talent headquarters. Its distinctive blue, red and yellow stands out above the other marquees along the cluttered strip. One panel, almost as large as the lettering itself, has a very stylish picture of the star herself as the logo. This and all the retail buildings throughout the metropolitan area that house businesses are consistent in design: modern, clean, white. They are attractive—like the picture, like Barbara herself.

All in all, it is undeniably a strong business concept. The public is buying the singer's image as much as the services provided. And that has basically been Barbara's formula for business success all through her career. She understands the value of making the customers feel they are getting a quality product. Whether it's entertainment or having photos developed in a few minutes, the principle is the same. The consumer of Mandrell's services feels satisfied, not ripped off. She is a merchant who gives fair value for a dollar, in itself a rarity of modern commerce. And shoppers in the market for whatever she has to offer seem to be in agreement: They like it, and they pay good money for it, over and over again.

10

Behind the Scenes &
Bouncing Back

ANNE BAKER WORKS at the Village Market, which is almost directly across from the entrance to subdivision number one. Here the street going back to Barbara Mandrell's house empties out onto Gallatin Road. The grocery clerk has often seen Barbara as she stops in late at night on the way to a concert. "They will pull in on a Sunday evening real late on their way out to a concert somewhere. She pulls off to the side in their tour bus and they wait until the store is pretty well empty. They buy some stuff like Cokes and bread just to carry on the trip with them. A few of them come off the bus to buy.

"Her yachtsman comes in all the time. He's a pretty good looking guy. You'd never know who he was. He never mentions who he works for. Her bus driver comes in here too. Just regular folks. They act like typical next-door neighbors.

"This section of road we're on is named Barbara Mandrell Boulevard. The day it was dedicated, you'd not believe the number of people, dignitaries. They stopped in here at the store, to get a Coke. One of them was the Mayor. He commented that it was one of the best things he had ever done in his life.

"Her people came from Westmoreland, Tennessee, originally. There's a lot of Mandrells that live up in Westmoreland and just about all of them can trace kin to her. That's just about twenty miles up the road. Stay straight on the highway and you'll run right into it.

"Most of her people are from right around this area. It's a family that's been here for years. It's like a citizen that has done good and brought fame to the county instead of a citizen that's done something bad. The city was glad to name the highway for her."

Several hundred people turned out in 1983 for the dedication ceremonies Anne Baker spoke of. The 1.7-mile stretch of Highway 31 East is between Volunteer State Community College and the Church of Christ in the country hamlet of number one.

As always, on that occasion the star gushed with superlatives. It's a part of her personality, reflecting her basic optimism. The syrupy accolades are also part of her public signature. "It's the greatest day of my life," said Barbara. "This takes the cake. Many of my family and friends traveled very far to be here. I'm so privileged to have them here. It's their moment too. I truly have never lived in a community that had more allegiance and pride. I plan to live out my days in Sumner County."

She tearfully reminisced about her grandfather Albert Anthony Mandrell. "He was born February 18, 1872, outside of Westmoreland. He was a proud, handsome man who loved Sumner County and the Grand Ole Opry. How we touch and affect others was important to him. That's what it's all about."

The strip of highway was marked with cross-shaped markers on the north and south ends of the designated stretch. A plaque on one reads:

This Section of Highway is Dedicated to Barbara Mandrell in Recognition of Her Professional Achievements and Her Admirable Personal Qualities. Barbara Mandrell Epitomizes the Name "Tennessean" and Portrays a Wholesome Image Which Brings Pride to Our City, County and State. June 9, 1983. The Citizens of Gallatin, Tenn.

Anne Patton, the executive secretary of the Chamber of Commerce, explained how the project got off the ground. "The Chamber of Commerce and the city of Gallatin did not originate this idea. About a year and a half ago, we were approached by some citizens who felt that because of her achievements, Gallatin should do something to recognize Mandrell. We had to get permission from the State Department of Transportation. They had to approve the design and location of the signs."

The zoning administrator for the city, Bobby Alkin, was also involved. He explained the physics of the tribute, which seem fitting in view of the honoree's close brush with death. "The signs are nine feet tall and two feet in width, with a hollow core. They have breakaway legs in case they are hit by a car. Both will be on state highway property." Bobby helped design the distinctive markers. The signs are made of redwood and the words BARBARA MANDRELL BOULEVARD are carved in them and painted yellow. In many ways the image of Barbara as a superstar doesn't quite work here. Hollywood glamor is out of place in this relatively rural setting. Barbara is comfortable with that more down-to-earth style, and the fans appreciate her genuineness. Despite her wealth, she has chosen to live out her life not far from where her family has resided for generations.

This is an area of rolling hills. Farms and fences dot the countryside, along with lakes created by the TVA system, which feeds the nearby Tennessee River. The rich pasture land is alive with horses and cows, and picturesque barns are scattered over the landscape along the spacious four-lane leading back to Hendersonville.

The lifestyle Barbara lives is really the best of both worlds. She has the countryside, the spacious world of the landed gentry. She also has her retreat on the lake, complete with a seventy-two-foot yacht. The *Lady Encore* is berthed at the docks below her home. It is an ocean-going vessel, painted in pink and peach, Barbara's favorite colors. The massive hull cuts the lake water gracefully, and the yacht has room for over thirty people to sunbathe on the upper deck. She and the family take trips to Florida and exotic ports around the lake. It is the essence of being rich and famous.

Barbara now seems ready to push herself in new directions. Her acting skill is helping her to broaden an already varied career. She is gaining more recognition in this area as her dramatic roles increase in number and dimension.

Back in 1982, before the accident, she was already talking to the press about her desire to appear in films. "I'm seriously going to do a movie—no doubt. I can still do one hundred road days a year and two movies in addition."

She explained why she had been reluctant to commit herself to other offers so far. "I think unnecessary violence and vulgar language is ridiculous, and I don't want to be associated with it. I had to turn down a marvelous opportunity—a character which was somebody I wanted to play—because I could not compromise what I consider to be good taste.

"So when the right one comes along, I'm sure it's going to have some cuss words in it, but they're going to be ones that really have to be there, where it would be noticeable if they weren't.

"So, yes, I'm going to do a movie, but, yes, I just turned down one that I was going to do in the next few months. So now if I do one, the way I'm letting my year fill in—because I've been away from the fans and I intend to get back out there on the road—I guess I can't do it until next winter."

The right one finally came along. And it came just when she had predicted—in early 1984. Ironically, it debuted simultaneously with the news of her auto accident.

The film was *Coalfire*. The story line had Mandrell playing a government geologist who comes to an Appalachian mining town in an attempt to put out a coalfire in the bedrock below. The raging fire threatens to destroy the small community. The D.C. scientist comes on the scene and meets a handsome wildlife agent played by Tom Wopat.

She had never acted before. Wopat, former star of *Dukes of Hazzard*, commented on her skills as a thespian: "She has excellent instincts and a great attitude." The author of the screenplay, Clifford Campion, agreed with that assessment. He added, "She's just wonderful."

The filming was done near Lake City in her home state. The coal region is about 130 miles due east of her home.

During the shooting, Barbara was confident and optimistic. "The local people have made it very comfortable for all of us. I hope I'm good at it so I can do more. It's really fun and interesting and totally different than anything else I've done."

The only difficulty came when she had a romantic scene

with Wopat. The kissing proved to be tough. Ken was standing nearby, and she began to giggle. She recalled, "Everything was going fine until our faces got to within a couple of inches of each other and I looked into those big blue eyes and just lost it.

"At least he is talented and handsome. All my girlfriends will be jealous."

Ken understood the problem and tried to put her at ease. He called for her to "act like a grown-up and quit giggling."

The residents of Lake City were glad for the attention Mandrell and company brought them. The 1,923 residents were excited to be able to see the two stars, along with costars Eddie Albert and Carol Kane.

Her second film opportunity came from the same man who produced her first movie. Gil Cates sent her a copy of the book *Burning Rage,* which had been adapted as a screenplay. She first read it several months before her accident and was very impressed.

The story involves a divorcée in Columbus, Ohio, who has a nine-year-old son. She and the boy are just starting to recover from the failure of her marriage. Barbara's character has a job on a local talk show, and is paying the bills for the first time. She is also getting some recognition on her own and finding that she enjoys it.

The son goes out to play one day, while his mother relaxes with a book. She hears a loud bang outside, followed by a siren. A police officer comes to the front door just as her son is walking in the back, covered with blood.

It seems that one of the older children brought a pistol out to show the other kids. The son and a friend tussle over the pistol and the friend is accidentally shot and killed. The community outrage that follows results in harassment of both mother and son, and even her job is threatened.

It wasn't difficult for her to play the mother's part in

Burning Rage because the character was someone she could like. She was strong and intelligent, yet feminine, giving and unselfish. And she held a position most often thought of as a man's job. There are more than a few similarities between Barbara and her character.

She has compared her transition from songstress to actress to a dream, or living another person's life. She got along well with Gil Cates, and respects his knowledge and ability. That he is also a gentleman earned him extra points with Barbara. He treated her well, and she appreciates it. Cates will probably also produce her next movie, when and if she finds the right screenplay.

Barbara points out that it was her husband who was the actor of the family. Ken had studied drama in college, and memorization has always been easy for him. Acting was easier than she had expected, under Gil Cates's tutelage. Gil taught her it is best to read a script through two or three times and leave memorizing lines until after a read-out at the day's shooting.

Whether Barbara will have the same success on screen as on record remains to be seen. The talent is certainly there, if a little raw. Her acting notices have been good, and the challenge is not one she is likely to run away from. The accident has delayed her expansion in this direction, but it is likely to claim an increasing share of her attention as her recovery progresses and her confidence returns.

Her recovery imposed on her time for reflection, and also seems to have given her a deeper sense of history. Always generous with her homage to direct influences, she has recently taken it a step further, expressing a debt of gratitude to the women who blazed trails in the country music business before her. She feels honored when she sees her name mentioned along with Kitty Wells, Minnie

Pearl, Rose Maddox and Patsy Cline, all of whom she admired and from all of whom she learned so much.

One of the outstanding country music ladies Barbara admires most is Dolly Parton. She selected her as the person with whom she would make her return to the stage after her accident. It was to be a special comeback tour.

Sponsored by Marlboro Country Music, the opening concert of the tour was to be held at the Universal Amphitheatre in Los Angeles. The *Star* (February 4, 1986) reported on the preparations. Barbara told Norma Langley, "I'm coming back because my heart is bursting with love for the friends who keep sending me messages of encouragement. . . . The only way I can think of to say thanks is to get back out there and be strong for them."

She admitted she was frightened, and that for the first time in her career she had stage fright. It had been a year and a half since the accident, and being away from the stage for so long a time had eroded her confidence. She was worried about her ankle and how her fans would react to the changes in her show that the injury had made necessary. The changes were designed to make the performances less physically demanding. Barbara also began to work out in a gym to increase her stamina.

Ken gave the *Star* some additional details: "We've contracted with Electro-Tech, who does Lionel Richie and Bette Midler's shows. They're building ramps instead of stairs. Barbara can't go down stairs with that ankle. She doesn't know how she's going to stage the show yet, because she doesn't know how long the ankle will hold up. She won't be doing any dancing like she used to, unless we can strengthen the ankle. . . . Her sister Louise is helping out with costuming. Barbara's still got the most important part of her show—her music. She's scared, but we know she's got more talent and creativity in her little finger than most people have in their whole bodies.''

In the same story, Barbara added: ''I know because I've thought about it a lot. By the time I'm into my third number on my first show, if I'm good enough, I'll feel great. . . . I'm sharing the truth with you. After the accident, when I realized it was going to take a long time to get back on my feet, I felt pretty sorry for myself. I used to be a tomboy. I never fully appreciated how strong I was. Then I woke up flat on my back and had to stay that way for a long time.''

Not surprisingly, the concert was a sellout. Six thousand faithful welcomed her back after an eighteen-month absence. She performed many of her oldies, much to the crowd's delight. The usual array of big names in show business were there: Jim Nabors, Tammy Wynette, Morgan Fairchild and Michele Lee, to name just a handful.

Barbara always says a prayer with the band before going on. This night, she felt more nervous than usual. After the prayer, she felt a sudden peace wash over her, and knew immediately that everything would be fine, even before stepping on stage to sing her first number.

She said later her ''biggest problem was keeping from crying when I saw all those familiar faces out in the audience. . . . My ankle's a little sore right now, but I'm grateful to the people who believed in me, encouraged me and who are now with me. I'm grateful that the only feelings that matter are happiness and love.''

She told her co-star beforehand she was worried the fans would no longer love her. Dolly said later, ''I told her she must have hurt her head real bad in that accident if she thought that.''

When Barbara tried to thank her for the tribute, Parton replied, ''Shucks, honey, I just did it for the money.''

Tammy Wynette flew in from Nashville to support her friend. Barbara didn't know it until after the concert. Talking to the press later, Wynette said: "I made the trip to show we care. After my last surgery, I was feeling pretty down. Barbara came by the hospital in Florida and just held my hand. . . . Last time I talked with her, she was very worried about having to slow down her dancing. Maybe she's moving around less than she used to, but she's more dynamic tonight than ninety-nine percent of the stars on two good legs."

Barbara explained how she managed with the injured limb. She had six costumes designed to accommodate six special pairs of boots with a brace built into the right ankle. Before she put them on, she had to wrap the ankle in a bandage. The doctor has told her to keep the leg elevated as much as she can and to apply heat if the pain gets bad.

It is that kind of dedication to her craft that makes Barbara Mandrell so special. It is also, and not coincidentally, what makes her so successful. And, despite the physical strains of the comeback tour, and all of the psychological stress that accompanied it, she managed to lighten things up with self-deprecating humor.

She observed to a post-concert gathering of journalists that, "My shoes and earrings don't match, and my hair looks like I stuck my finger in a light bulb—but I'm hip. It's like making a silk purse out of a sow's ear."

The concert's star also had a surprise visit from Lee Greenwood, who sang "To Me" in a duet with her. The two had just finished a recording of the tune and he came especially to perform it for the opening-night crowd.

Afterward, interviewed by the press, Barbara's peers gave her accolades.

Suzanne Somers said, "She must be the bravest human being I've ever known."

Pat Boone was there too. He remarked, "Barbara Mandrell is what show business should be all about. Now that she's back, the heart is back in country music."

Barbara herself said that she thanked God every day for letting her make the comeback, and that, if she could, she'd like personally to thank every person who sent get-well messages and gifts to her. She knows she can't do that, but she *can* tour and let the fans see how much they've helped her. She decided to call it the "Get to the Heart" tour because she felt she had been given the strength to come back by the dedication of her fans. The rest of the tour would last about two months. They hadn't planned more than that because of a movie commitment. And Barbara was still facing surgery for removal of a pin from her leg, later in the summer.

Having a new baby presented its own set of problems, but she seemed to be coping well with them. She found the new baby to be no trouble on the tour, and thinks that he made it even more fun. Already a great traveler, he's his mother's son, and Barbara finds it a comfort to know he's close by.

She and Ken work things out so that one of them is always with the children. They work hard at being a family team, and Barbara says she feels lucky to be married to her best friend.

Barbara is warm. She cares about her fans. Casting her bread upon the waters, she puts it out there and it just keeps coming back. She was interviewed on the Oprah Winfrey show in 1987 in what was as personal and in-depth an interview as any she has done. Ken appeared with her, and the two gave a perspective on her life and career from a unique behind-the-scenes vantage point.

Barbara observed that when you love people, they love you back. She talked at length about her belief in God, and the personal vision of her relationship with Him. While she doesn't necessarily know what He wants for her, she still puts things in His hands, and they seem to go well. It is not easy to explain why she has had such trials, but she feels she's learned from them.

The first, and most obvious, thing that comes to her mind is how readily we take our health for granted. She had never really thought about her own health, and how precarious a thing it is, but now she is truly grateful when she has a day without pain.

She told Oprah and the audience how helpful both her neurosurgeon and her minister had been after the accident. They are the only people with whom she has been able to talk about it to any degree. It is difficult for her still, and she becomes very emotional.

The accident seems to have changed a lot of things for her. She no longer looks at life the same way. The stage fright before her comeback concert is just one manifestation of her altered outlook. The confident, carefree performer was suddenly scared of facing her audience and trying to entertain them.

She also admitted that the public response to her return to performing has continued to amaze her. The support was a great help to her. She finds it difficult to describe the full impact of that devotion. Letters and cards, flowers and gifts poured in from all over America, some even from other parts of the world.

Barbara seems to have a new candor since the accident. Under Winfrey's questioning, she went on to discuss her drive, her dreams and her goals. She believes you shouldn't take no for an answer. Despite this drive, she feels you should not hurt anybody along the way, because she knows the way you treat people and the way you conduct your business can come back to haunt you and you will be repaid in kind.

She claims she is never satisfied. And that dissatisfaction with limits is what allows you to do more. She even extends that philosophy to her private life. It was evident from the show that Barbara has been thinking a great deal about her life. She now says that she is a better mother than she is a wife. She seems to have developed a newfound respect for her husband. She sang his praises to Oprah and found herself in some rough water.

She is not a feminist, and, as usual, tried to avoid anything controversial in her responses. She managed to articulate a theory of sexual equality that would not satisfy supporters of the ERA but that reflects the kind of equality she and Ken have managed to build into their complicated lives.

Ken confided that for part of his married life people had referred to him as "Mr. Mandrell." He told Oprah that was fine with him as long as Barbara brings the money home. His reputation for humor was proving to be accurate. He likes to joke that his wife goes out and makes the money and he spends it.

Barbara disputed his self-deprecatory remarks. The truth, as she sees it, is that Ken is an exceptional businessman. She believes they managed to survive her eighteen-month layoff as a result of his shrewd business management.

Ken explained it by reminding her that he sold newspapers and did gardening work as a kid. Later on, he worked in a hardware store while going to college and playing in Irby's band. He teasingly said that Irby never paid enough, so he had to work at other jobs to make ends meet.

He claimed to have been another Clint Eastwood until he married Barbara. His tone changed when talking about it. He was suddenly very intent. Ken articulated his attitude toward marriage with passion and intelligence. His view was considerably more enlightened than one might expect from a ''country boy.'' Equality and sharing the responsibilities are the two most important considerations for him.

The need to reciprocate affection, to be nicer to her family, is something that has become more important to Barbara. According to Ken, she became so dependent upon him after the accident that she wouldn't let anyone else help her in and out of bed.

Barbara was angry during that time, but now she can't recall the full extent of her rage. On the Winfrey program, she claimed she was ''horrible'' to be around. But Ken defended her: ''If you live with pain on a daily basis and the amounts that she had, you really, really, have problems. And I'm really starting to appreciate now, even after two years, what she has gone through, with the therapy she did and all the pain and suffering and depression. She has done a marvelous, marvelous job. And I really appreciate that.''

Barbara agreed with Ken's explanation of her behavior. ''When you're hurting you don't care. You just want to not hurt. And you really don't miss or care about anything.'' She was sincere and her eyes showed the pain.

She does care. She has battled the pain. She has been working relentlessly on new goals even before her return. She has just signed with Capitol/EMI American records. The reborn star anticipates a number of new projects from them.

She has been busy making a television special about youth and family problems. This was sponsored by Youth for Christ, an international evangelical youth organization. Filming was done in Franklin, Tennessee. Ken flew in, piloting a custom helicopter. "I always come along to kind of protect her from autograph hounds. Her work is hard enough as it is."

Not only is the work hard, but Barbara works hard at it. Always on the move, she never seems to have quite accomplished her goals. She is looking to future achievement, such as acting. Her stage background gives her the necessary skills to step over into this related field.

The specifics never seem to matter to her. She just sets her goal, moves in and begins to adapt and master the skills. This represents a remarkable versatility and Barbara has a keen sense of her abilities. In one sense, she knows no limitations. Someone once said that if your goals don't scare you, they probably aren't high enough. If she's scared, it doesn't show for the most part. She is a good actor. Maybe that's part of the role she's playing. But no one's ever been able to get through to her that there is something she might *not* be able to accomplish. Even in the face of tragedy.

Beneath the somewhat Pollyanna exterior is a core of smooth steel. It is highly polished and razor-sharp. She is still, as ever, ready to conquer the unknown. She keeps climbing. This passion for exploration, for expansion of her talent, explains why there will be much more success in her future. Succeeding is the one thing she does best, followed closely by inspiring hundreds of thousands to excel by her example.

America needs heroes and heroines. Now, more than ever, Barbara Mandrell comes as close as anyone to filling that need. She champions the common person, not only through her music but in her personal life. As with anyone seen close up, her flaws, however minor, begin to show. But in spite of the blemishes, there is really no one better at doing what she does, no one better able to make people feel good about themselves. In some ways, she is an anachronism, a throwback to a simpler time. But a drift back to that simpler time has been a strong current in the national mood lately. Things have been a bit out of control for most Americans, as if the national psyche has been in a tailspin. If people need Barbara to show them they too can pull themselves out, then let her go to it. She's best at making people feel comfortable, entertained, optimistic . . . and just plain proud to know her.

11

The Future

WHAT DOES THE future hold for Barbara Mandrell and her family? Has she accomplished it all before she even reaches her fortieth birthday?

She has money, looks and fame. Adoring fans by the thousands cheer her at every performance. Managing to have a successful career and a solid family life is itself no small accomplishment in modern America. When the career is in show business, the achievement is all the more remarkable. Her family is ideally suited for a woman with her drive—a supportive husband and adaptable kids. She lives in a fine home, drives high-end automobiles and even has a yacht. She is blessed with a wide variety of friends from all walks of life, not a few of them in high places. She even has her own museum. If there is anything she lacks, it's sufficient space to display the trophies, awards and other accolades bestowed on her by the dozen.

She has seen and done it all, from the highest highs to the lowest lows. She had triumphed over the despair and desolation of a serious injury. She has endured its agonizing pain and that of major surgery. Months of isolation and separation from the fans that constitute her world have been unable to dampen her enthusiasm for life, let alone break her spirit. Her reality is as close to the American ideal as one can get.

Barbara has struck gold in every area of entertainment she has touched. She has a national fan club of paid members ten thousand strong. She is a regular on the People's Choice awards. For many, she has come to symbolize an America the less idealistic among us thought dead and buried.

The Grand Ole Opry stage, which at one time must have seemed like the pinnacle, now is just one small piece in the mosaic of her entertainment life. She has gone far, far beyond the boundaries that confine most kids with her background. She has rewritten a few rules on what women are supposed to do and what a country singer is supposed to be like. She shatters records and stereotypes, yet with it all somehow manages to keep her down-home values. She is the epitome of an old-fashioned girl of the heartland. Barbara Mandrell is just the girl next door, trying to make a living like the rest of us.

Judging by the mass of awards and records she has accumulated, it is safe to say she is part of the national consciousness. People hum her tunes as they drive to work or walk through the nation's shopping malls. Her impact on TV and the media has been a reflection of a deeper movement toward a conservative tone in this country. The image of the strong nuclear family has been resurgent in recent years. The Osmonds were a good example of the first stirrings; the Mandrells have brought it even farther. Their own closeness as a family helped knit a bond with the public. The success of *Family Ties* and *The Cosby*

Show demonstrates that the movement has yet to run its course. It is difficult to say whether Barbara Mandrell has played a significant role in that movement, or merely been in step with it.

The unabashed willingness of the singer to express her belief in God and her profound expression of faith in Jesus Christ have made her nearly unique among major entertainment figures. They have also endeared her to the conservative Christian masses. In this regard, only Pat Boone comes to mind as a precursor.

Barbara's commitment to quality is one of the single greatest contributions she has made to her craft. Whether to try new technology on stage or in the studio, or to achieve perfection in performance on record and on tour, the results have been the same. The country music industry is the better for her consummate professionalism. Rarely is it possible to find anyone willing to go the distance just to get it perfect. She does.

She has also shown the nation something of courage. Her bravery during her crisis was inspiring. Many people, when confronted with great pain on a continuing basis, might have succumbed to the temptations of medication, but not Barbara Mandrell. She fought back and, through sheer willpower, resisted the seduction. Her struggle was all the more inspiring because it was neither tainted by any suggestion of decadence nor the result of willful abuse of "recreational" drugs, as indulged in by the endless parade of celebrity junkies, juicers and pill-poppers who march to and from the Betty Ford Center.

There is a debit side to the Mandrell ledger, however. Her efforts at being nice seem so real, so warm. At times, the smile might be contrived. She must occasionally feel exhaustion, fear or loneliness but, if so, they are tightly reined, perpetually masked behind the cloak of exuberance. But even if sometimes feigned, the veneer is so gallant that it might as well be real. And people flock to her in spite of her slightly unreal world view, or, perhaps, because of it.

The amazing devotion from her fans is moving, especially that of the dues-paying variety. The fees to join must be worth it to them. In return, they get a "fix" of Mandrell intimacy: snapshots and XOXOXOXOX's at the bottom of her letters. She is unabashedly sentimental, but what might be a liability to a more sophisticated audience has instead become her trademark.

The substance of an April 1986 fan letter is an example. In it, she tells the fans that she and the family, except for Nathaniel, are going on vacation for the spring break from school. They are planning on two solid weeks of fun with one another. They will leave the youngest with an aunt. She laments the prospect of being away from her son for so long, but he is not yet old enough for swimming and fishing. She closes with a note that she will tell the fans all about the vacation in the next newsletter, and warns them that it will probably be a long one.

The media generation seems to have the feeling it is on a first-name basis with any celebrity. It is possible, therefore, to argue that Barbara has created a potential monster. An aggressive public is unpredictable at best, at worst dangerous. Every crowd might have its Mark David Chapman or John Hinckley. This is the reason very few public notables do it the way Barbara has done it. Of course, this is also the reason she has brought down the awards consistently. But, with children to worry about, Barbara seems more worldly, more realistic about security now. Not necessarily a crack in the mask, it nevertheless represents a retreat from her earlier attitude toward her public.

The concern for her fans also sets another trap for her.

The desire to play to its taste requires a nod in the direction of the least common denominator. Since Barbara—and, by extension, her audience—is deathly afraid of controversy, pulpy information has to be fed to it, and her art adjusted to please a broad spectrum of taste. This version of reality is cut with a dose of syrup. It's not bad, since it's far too professional for that. But too much leaves a sticky taste in some mouths. It also creates the suspicion that she can't be for real. No one can be that good, that nice. Or can they?

Close examination leaves many questions unanswered. Where are the frustrations of Mandrell's everyday human experience, the problems? Do the Dudneys never have any? It seems so unbalanced. Only the very best of news, all with smiles and flowers, flows from the Mandrell presses. The full range of expression seems abridged, half the range of human emotions seems to be missing.

While it would be very uncomfortable for everyone if the star were to go around emoting heavily, on occasion it would be refreshing to see her newsletter say, for example, "I was a bear today. Had a massive headache. I yelled at Ken and the kids. They all went out and left me alone." This is the kind of stuff one will never see in the newsletter. Barbara is an entertainer. People expect to be entertained, so she gives 'em what they want to hear.

Of all the paradoxes that confront a person trying to understand the Mandrell phenomenon, perhaps the most telling is this: the enormous distance needed to operate a "close to the fan" operation. Even Barbara's publicist has an assistant, so that one has to go through the assistant to get to the publicist so that one can put in a request to get to Mandrell. Not surprisingly, the gates swing shut if it seems the domain is threatened. The moat around the castle is sufficiently wide that only managed news about its inhabitants makes it out into the world.

But it's a paradox that Barbara takes in her stride. Like everyone else, she seems to have a life filled with little ironies. "She Was Country When Country Wasn't Cool." Yet, she was "Cool and Never Quite Country." Her music is bluesy and black, with a hint of jazz. In fact, many critics thought she was too far from the norm to be a true country singer.

She is a star from Nashville, who dresses with the flair of Beverly Hills. She is glamorous and poised. Gone now are the homespun ways that still drape many of her peers and that were part of her appeal in the very earliest days. Simplicity has been replaced by studied elegance. In retrospect, it is hard to say if she ever truly had a backwoods flavor about her. She was from California. She might have given the impression of down home, but underneath, possibly even at twelve or thirteen, the future Queen of Crossover was already peeking through the blinds.

Another contradiction, the one that most troubles her fundamentalist fans, is indicative of the sophistication she has developed. She grew up in a church that denounced the sins of the flesh, yet ninety-nine percent of Barbara's songs are flirting with those very sins. The titles of her songs say it all: "Married, But Not to Each Other," "If Lovin' You Is Wrong I Don't Want to Be Right," "Playing Around With Love." For many, she is the very word on family togetherness and harmony. Yet the "Cheatin' Song" makes up most of her repertoire.

Obviously, commercial considerations come into play in the choice of material, but there is a broader context to consider as well, and one suspects that much of her audience has, at one time or another, regardless of religious beliefs, been confronted with the kinds of moral dilemmas that, if we are to take Barbara's image at face value, exist for her only on vinyl.

As hard as she has worked at creating a cosmetic image, at times the real person shows through. The most intriguing thing about such lapses, however, is that the face under the mask does not appear to be that different from the mask it hides behind. Barbara Mandrell may very well be just what she seems to be. But one can't avoid wondering why, if that is so, she needs a mask at all.

Where can she go from here? Her current level of popularity is so high, it would seem to be impossible to sustain it for long. She is still relatively young. But ten, or even twenty, years from now, will her museum still be viable? Will she still command the People's Choice Award, or fill a concert hall? The answer is probably. There's something about her that's unexplainable. Her very contact with the audiences seems to rejuvenate her. She will endure, most likely, as long as she wants to. People need and like Barbara Mandrell. They respond to something in her, get something from her, that no other performer seems to have.

And the Mandrell family industry seems likely to continue as well. Given her own past, it is a good bet she will propel her children down the path she cleared. Matt's already taking guitar lessons. Jaime's doing voice-over for the photo shops in Nashville. The kids have had a wealth of exposure to the stage and its stars. They have learned about publicity and speaking from their mother. The role models they enjoy for parents are exceptional. They may even form their own group. A sharp eye will probably be able to pick Barbara out of the background in her later years.

But the future depends on whether she can keep from getting bored. A driven dynamo like Barbara has to keep raising her sights to survive. She is an adrenaline-soaked workaholic. She needs the challenge to continue working. But what is left for her: to continue to sing the same songs, to continue to entertain the same people with the same material, however highly polished? Or should she look for new fields to conquer?

Whatever she might decide, don't count her out. She's a fighter. She'll be in the public eye as long as there's a publicist around to crank out the word. Barbara Mandrell has walked away from the wreckage, she's back, and she's better than ever!

Discography

Singles

| --- | --- | --- |
7/22/69	Columbia	*I've Been Lovin' You Too Long/ Baby Come Home*
4/14/70	Columbia	*Playing Around With Love/ I Almost Lost My Mind*
12/31/70	Columbia	*Do-Right Woman/Do-Right Man/The Letter*
5/20/71	Columbia	*Treat Him Right/Break My Mind*
11/4/71	Columbia	*Tonight My Baby's Coming Home/ He'll Never Take the Place of You*
3/17/72	Columbia	*Show Me/Satisfied*

9/22/72	Columbia	*Holdin' On (To the Love I Got)/ Smile, Somebody Loves You*
3/16/73	Columbia	*Give a Little, Take a Little/ Ain't It Good*
7/13/73	Columbia	*The Midnight Oil/In the Name of Love*
5/17/74	Columbia	*This Time I Almost Made It/ Son-of-a-Gun*
11/75	Dot/ABC	*Standing Room Only/Can't Help But Wonder*
3/76	Dot/ABC	*That's What Friends Are For/ The Beginning of the End*
7/76	Dot/ABC	*Love Is Thin Ice/ Will We Ever Make Love in Love Again?*
11/76	Dot/ABC	*Midnight Angel/I Count You*
3/8/77	Dot/ABC	*Married, But Not to Each Other/ Fool's Gold*
8/77	Dot	*Hold Me/ This Is Not Another Cheatin' Song*
11/77	Dot	*Woman to Woman/Let the Rain Out*
4/6/78	ABC	*Tonight/If I Were a River*

8/1/78	ABC	*Sleeping Single in a Double Bed/* *Just One More*
1/79	ABC	*If Loving You Is Wrong, I Don't* *Want To Be Right/* *I Feel the Hurt Coming On*
7/79	MCA	*Fooled by a Feeling/* *Love Takes a Long Time to Die*
12/7/79	MCA	*Years/Darlin'*
6/6/80	MCA	*Crackers/Using Him to Get to You*
9/26/80	MCA	*The Best of Strangers/* *Sometime, Somewhere, Somehow*
1/23/81	MCA	*Love is Fair/* *Sometime, Somewhere, Somehow*
4/16/81	MCA	*I Was Country When Country* *Wasn't Cool/* *A Woman's Got a Right (To* *Change Her Mind)*
8/21/81	MCA	*Wish You Were Here/* *She's Out There Dancin' Alone*
4/8/82	MCA	*Till You're Gone/* *You're Supposed to Be Here*
8/12/82	MCA	*Operator/Black and White*
3/28/83	MCA	*In Times Like These/Loveless*

8/11/83	MCA	*One of a Kind, Pair of Fools/* *As Well As Can Be Expected*
2/1/84	MCA	*Happy Birthday, Dear Heartache/* *A Man's Not a Man (Till He's* *Loved by a Woman)*
5/24/84	MCA	*Only a Lonely Heart Knows/* *I Wonder What the Rich Folk Are* *Doin' Tonight*
6/25/84	MCA	*To Me (with Lee Greenwood)/* *We Were Meant for Each Other*
9/17/84	MCA	*Crossword Puzzle/* *If It's Not One Thing, It's Another*
11/26/84	MCA	*Santa, Bring My Baby Home/* *It Must Have Been the Mistletoe*
1/14/85	MCA	*It Should Have Been Love by Now/* *Can't Get Too Much of a Good* *Thing*
2/25/85	MCA	*There's No Love in Tennessee/* *Sincerely I'm Yours*
7/29/85	MCA	*Angel in Your Arms/* *Don't Look in My Eyes*
11/18/85	MCA	*Fast Lanes and Country Roads/* *You, Only You*
3/86	MCA	*When You Get to the Heart (with* *The Oak Ridge Boys)/Survivors*

7/86	MCA	*No One Mends a Broken Heart Like You/Love Is Adventure in The Great Unknown*
6/87	Capitol/EMI-America	*Child Support/I'm Glad I Married You*
10/87	Capitol	*Angels Love Bad Men (with Waylon Jennings)/Sunshine Street*

Albums

RELEASE	LABEL	TITLE
9/71	Columbia	*Treat Him Right*
11/73	Columbia	*The Midnight Oil*
8/74	Columbia	*This Time I Almost Made It*
1/76	Dot	*This Is Barbara Mandrell*
9/76	Dot	*Midnight Angel*
8/77	Columbia	*The Best of Barbara Mandrell*
8/77	ABC/Dot	*Lovers, Friends & Strangers*
3/78	ABC/Dot	*Love's Ups and Downs*
9/78	ABC	*Moods*
3/79	ABC	*The Best of Barbara Mandrell*

7/79	MCA	*Just for the Record*
8/80	MCA	*Love is Fair*
7/81	Columbia	*Looking Back*
8/81	MCA	*Barbara Mandrell Live*
5/82	MCA	*In Black and White*
9/82	MCA/Songbird	*He Set My Life to Music*
7/83	MCA	*Spun Gold*
4/84	MCA	*Clean Cut*
7/84	MCA	*Meant for Each Other (with Lee Greenwood)*
10/84	MCA	*Christmas at Our House*
3/85	MCA	*Barbara Mandrell's Greatest Hits*
8/85	MCA	*Get to the Heart*
7/87	Capitol/EMI-America	*Sure Feels Good*

Duet Singles With David Houston

RELEASE	LABEL	TITLE
9/2/70	Epic	*After Closing Time/My Song of Love*

8/23/71	Epic	*We've Got Everything But Love/* *Try a Little Harder*
8/16/72	Epic	*A Perfect Match/Almost Persuaded*
11/21/73	Epic	*I Love You, I Love You/* *Let's Go Down Together*
4/19/74	Epic	*Lovin' You Is Worth It/* *How Can It Be Wrong?*
7/12/74	Epic	*Ten Commandments of Love/* *Try a Little Harder*

Duet Albums With David Houston

RELEASE	LABEL	TITLE
8/72	Epic	*A Perfect Match*
4/74	Epic	*The Best of Barbara Mandrell and David Houston*